To My Darling Francy

Happy Birthday Sweetheart. Better late than never.
I know you will have lots of fun with this book I'm looking
forward especially to the bread.

Love You Forever
Your Keith
xxxx

1990

COMBINATION ◆MICROWAVE◆
C·O·O·K·B·O·O·K

COMBINATION
MICROWAVE
C·O·O·K·B·O·O·K

BRIDGET JONES

HAMLYN

CONTENTS

Copyright © The Hamlyn Publishing Group Limited 1987

Published by the Hamlyn Publishing Group Limited,
a division of the Octopus Publishing Group,
Michelin House,
81 Fulham Road,
London SW3 6RB

First published 1987

Second impression 1989

Photography by James Murphy
Line drawings by Jane Brewster

ISBN 0 600 32705 1

Set in Monophoto Optima by Servis Filmsetting Ltd, Manchester

Produced by Mandarin Offset
Printed in Hong Kong

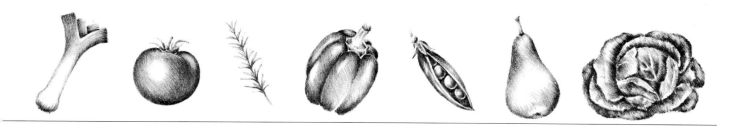

◆

For Mam and Dad,
to go with their newest
kitchen appliance.

◆

*The author and publishers would like to thank the following
for lending ovens for testing purposes:*
Belling and Co. Ltd., Hitachi Sales UK Ltd., Hotpoint Ltd., Jones and Brother Ltd.,
Panasonic UK Ltd., Sanyo Marubeni Ltd., Sharp Electronics Ltd., Siemens
Domestic Appliances and Toshiba (UK) Ltd. Thanks are also due to T.I. Creda
Limited for testing sample recipes in their appliance.

♦ USEFUL FACTS ♦
AND FIGURES

Notes on metrication

In this book quantities are given in metric and Imperial measures. Exact conversion from Imperial to metric measures does not usually give very convenient working quantities and so the metric measures have been rounded off into units of 25 grams. The table below shows the recommended equivalents.

Ounces	Approx g to nearest whole figure	Recommended conversion to nearest unit of 25	Ounces	Approx g to nearest whole figure	Recommended conversion to nearest unit of 25
1	28	25	9	255	250
2	57	50	10	283	275
3	85	75	11	312	300
4	113	100	12	340	350
5	142	150	13	368	375
6	170	175	14	396	400
7	198	200	15	425	425
8	227	225	16 (1 lb)	454	450

Note: When converting quantities over 16 oz first add the appropriate figures in the centre column, then adjust to the nearest unit of 25. As a general guide, 1 kg (1000 g) equals 2.2 lb or about 2 lb 3 oz. This method of conversion gives good results in nearly all cases, although in certain pastry and cake recipes a more accurate conversion is necessary to produce a balanced recipe.

Liquid measures The millilitre has been used in this book and the following table gives a few examples.

Imperial	Approx ml to nearest whole figure	Recom- mended ml	Imperial	Approx ml to nearest whole figure	Recom- mended ml
$\frac{1}{4}$ pint	142	150 ml	1 pint	567	600 ml
$\frac{1}{2}$ pint	283	300 ml	1$\frac{1}{2}$ pints	851	900 ml
$\frac{3}{4}$ pint	425	450 ml	1$\frac{3}{4}$ pints	992	1000 ml (1 litre)

Spoon measures All spoon measures given in this book are level unless otherwise stated.

Can sizes At present, cans are marked with the exact (usually to the nearest whole number) metric equivalent of the Imperial weight of the contents, so we have followed this practice when giving can sizes.

Oven temperatures The table below gives recommended equivalents.

	°C	°F	Gas Mark		°C	°F	Gas Mark
Very cool	110	225	$\frac{1}{4}$	Moderately hot	190	375	5
	120	250	$\frac{1}{2}$		200	400	6
Cool	140	275	1	Hot	220	425	7
	150	300	2		230	450	8
Moderate	160	325	3	Very hot	240	475	9
	180	350	4				

Notes for American and Australian users

In America the 8-fl oz measuring cup is used. In Australia metric measures are now used in conjunction with the standard 250-ml measuring cup. The Imperial pint, used in Britain and Australia, is 20 fl oz, while the American pint is 16 fl oz. It is important to remember that the Australian tablespoon differs from both the British and American tablespoons; the table below gives a comparison. The British standard tablespoon, which has been used throughout this book, holds 17.7 ml, the American 14.2 ml, and the Australian 20 ml. A teaspoon holds approximately 5 ml in all three countries.

British	American	Australian
1 teaspoon	1 teaspoon	1 teaspoon
1 tablespoon	1 tablespoon	1 tablespoon
2 tablespoons	3 tablespoons	2 tablespoons
3$\frac{1}{2}$ tablespoons	4 tablespoons	3 tablespoons
4 tablespoons	5 tablespoons	3$\frac{1}{2}$ tablespoons

Key to symbols

◈ HIGH   Denotes use of microwaves only and the setting.

Combination:

◈ MEDIUM   Denotes combination of microwaves and

◆ 240 C   heat, giving setting and temperature.

♦ The above information appears next to the recipes.
♦ The first symbol is used **only** when a part of the recipe is cooked using microwaves only.
♦ The symbols under the *combination* heading tell you what microwave setting and temperature to select for the combination cooking mode.

Microwave settings

The following power levels apply to the different settings used in the recipes. In testing on combination mode little difference in cooking time was evident between 600W and 650W.

♦ HIGH   600W or 650W
♦ MEDIUM   350W or 360W
♦ LOW   180W

Temperature settings

♦ The temperature settings given in the recipes go up to 250 C.
♦ If the maximum temperature for your oven is 240 C, then use it instead of 250 C.
♦ If your oven has a limited number of temperature settings, then select the one nearest to the temperature given in the recipe. If necessary, use a lower temperature than that suggested instead of a hotter setting.

◆ FOREWORD ◆

With a combination microwave oven in your kitchen, dreams of having an oven that cooks significantly faster than normal but still gives the best results come true. I was very excited by the successes I achieved when I first started to cook in a microwave oven – indeed as I experimented, the disasters were just as useful as the winners because they pointed out the direction in which microwave cooking led. Take all those disasters, rethink them slightly and put them in a combination microwave and the chances are most of them will come out tops!

Making pies and cakes, bread and grills or roasting meat really did have me leaping around in the kitchen calling out to my husband to come and look at the latest great results from the combination microwave: I had, of course, anticipated that the combination of heat and microwaves would give good results but I was quite amazed at the quality of the results and speed with which the food cooked.

As I learnt how to use the ovens, there were one or two hints that I picked up, usually from my own errors. One thing that I found very difficult at first was to remember that the new appliance was very hot. Having cooked in an ordinary microwave oven for some time, as soon as the timer sounded to let me know that my recipe was ready I rushed over and on many occasions only just stopped myself before I grabbed the red-hot dish with my bare hands! So remember to use oven gloves. Another slight word of warning – the oven cavity itself (in most ovens) is quite small and the position in which the turntable stops can leave the handle of a dish towards the back of the oven, so do take care not to burn yourself on the sides of the oven as you try to remove the food – I suffered a few sore wrists from not bothering to turn a dish round on the rack before actually lifting it out.

As with many tabletop cooking appliances, the ovens do vary according to make, so I'm afraid that old phrase 'get used to your own oven' is relevant yet again. I always feel as though I'm cheating slightly when I tell people that they really do have to get to know their own oven and that this book will not do that for them, but it is true. For example, most manufacturers tell you not to preheat the oven before cooking and this is not just to promote the appliance as economical but because the cooking results are found to be superior if the food is cooked from cold. But I found that in many cases if the oven was not preheated the food did not have time to brown. In other cases, the oven heated up so quickly that I had to keep a very close watch on the food as it cooked to make sure it didn't burn.

Whatever the characteristics of your own oven are, I hope you find that the recipes in the chapters which follow will provide you with a repertoire of dishes that will cook successfully by this revolutionary new method. They were tested in a broad variety of ovens and I tried to balance out the instructions to guide you towards a good result no matter what model you own. Just remember that at first it is a good idea to watch the food as it cooks, keep a close eye on the time and don't be afraid to open the oven door – the microwaves will automatically stop!

As always, my chief taster and critic spent a lot of time in the kitchen making all the right, encouraging noises as I churned out the recipes, so credit is due to Neill for his input into the work involved in creating the book. Back in the office, Stella Vayne tackled the task of editing and correcting and at the photographic studio Nicola Diggins made the food for all the photographs.

I can only add that I really have thoroughly enjoyed discovering this wonderful new cooking method and I hope that you will find the recipes helpful. Most of all I hope you enjoy cooking in your new appliance and come to find it quite indispensible. Good luck and bon appétit!

Bridget Jones

◆ INTRODUCTION ◆

Combination Cooking – the Facts

Your combination microwave cooker is a versatile kitchen appliance, providing three alternative cooking methods: the food can be cooked by using microwaves only (as in any standard microwave oven), it can be cooked by traditional methods using the convection mode (fan-assisted oven), or it can be cooked on a combination mode, using the microwaves and heat together.

Combination Cooking Defined
Combination cooking is the method of cooking using microwave energy and conventional heat simultaneously. The majority of ovens offering this facility combine the microwave energy with recirculating hot air, produced by the high-speed fan built into the oven. In addition, some models have a grill built into the oven, in which case a combination of grilling and microwave cooking can be used for certain cooking procedures.

From the range of literature that is available on this cooking process you will find that many terms are used to describe the same cooking process. For example, you may find reference to a *convection microwave oven*, a *microwave-convection oven*, a *multi-micro cooker*, *microwave plus cookery*, *dual cooking* or *high-speed cooking*.

Whatever the term used, the exciting part of this cooking method is the results that can be achieved. Take all the time-tested standards of traditional cooking and marry them with the speed of cooking with microwaves: the result is the best of good cooking with the advantages of modern technology.

Recipes in this Book
This book concentrates on the simultaneous use of fan-assisted heat (convection cooking) with microwave energy, and it is this cooking mode which is used for all the recipes. The use of the grill in combination with microwaves is discussed on pages 13–14.

Combination Mode
In combination cookers the temperature settings are given in degrees centigrade (C). Throughout the book you will find the cooking temperature expressed in this way – if you want to convert back to Fahrenheit (F), then refer to **Useful Facts and Figures** on page 6. The range of cooking temperatures that can be selected varies according to the different ovens, however it is usually in the region of 140–250 C.

The microwave settings that can be used in combination with heat also vary from oven to oven. The majority of ovens allow for the use of high, medium or low microwave settings in combination with conventional heat. Some models limit the use of microwave settings to medium when using the combination cooking mode and other ovens offer high or low microwave settings. The majority of combination cooking is carried out on a medium microwave setting.

Some ovens are pre-programmed to provide a selection of different combinations of microwave energy and temperature settings; in this case you are limited in choice of temperature and microwave energy input. Pre-programmed ovens are discussed on page 13.

Advantages of Combination Cooking
By using microwaves the cooking process is speeded up and by using conventional heat the food turns brown and develops a crisp texture, or crust. Cooking by microwaves alone produces food with a steamed flavour – it is fair to say that microwave cooking is a moist cooking method. However, cooking by the combination method results in food which has a baked flavour.

Pastry, 'roast' meat and batters are a few examples of foods that are inferior or unacceptable when cooked by microwaves only. Cook these items by a combination of microwaves and conventional heat and the results are excellent – pastry becomes crisp, flaked and tasty with a brown crust; meat roasts very well, giving a traditional result in significantly less time than roasting by conventional means; and batters rise, become crisp and turn brown in a fraction of the time normally taken.

Breads and cakes rise too, cook through and have a crisp, browned crust. The taste is similar to that achieved by conventional methods.

Any recipes that require the food to be thoroughly heated or cooked through, with a crisp coating or browned topping are also particularly successful in the combination oven. While the crisp coating, or pastry pie lid, cooks and browns the food underneath cooks through without drying out.

Preheating the Oven for Combination Cooking
You will find most manufacturers state that it is not necessary to preheat the oven for combination cooking. In fact they suggest that results are better if the oven is not preheated. In some cases this is perfectly correct; however, when testing I found that in some ovens if the cooking time was short (and in many cases this is so) the food did not have time to

become crisp and well browned unless the oven was preheated. Results vary significantly from oven to oven – some ovens heat up very quickly, others can take up to 20 minutes. So, when it comes to preheating it really is a case of getting to know your own oven.

The recipes were tested in a preheated oven unless otherwise stated. When roasting meat or poultry, if the size of the food is large enough, there is no need to preheat. Try cooking a few dishes in your oven without preheating it first. If the results are not brown enough or not quite 'baked' enough then you will know it is necessary to preheat for any other recipe with a similar cooking time.

Microwave Cooking

All combination cookers can be used to cook by microwaves only. Any power setting available can be selected and the results will be the same as those achieved in any other standard microwave cooker. If you are not familiar with microwave cooking, then the following notes may be of some help. Remember always to read the manufacturer's instructions and to follow them.

Microwaves are non-ionising, electromagnetic waves, similar to radio waves. They pass straight through certain materials just as light passes straight through a window. The waves pass through glass, china and some plastics. Microwaves are reflected off metals or any highly glazed pottery. Food absorbs the microwaves.

When the waves hit food, they excite the water molecules (all food contains a certain amount of water) causing friction which in turn creates heat. It is this heat, produced within the food, that does the cooking. So when you hear that microwaves cook food 'from the inside' this is what is meant.

The waves are produced in the magnetron, then they travel into the oven cavity where they are distributed, usually by means of a stirrer located in the top of the oven. The waves bounce off the top, sides, base and specially designed door of the oven to hit the food from all sides. The waves will travel only 2.5– 5 cm/1–2 in into the food. When they have travelled as far as possible into the food and created a good deal of heat, any remaining uncooked food right in the centre is cooked by conduction, just as in conventional cooking methods. When possible, and if necessary, the food is stirred or rearranged during cooking so that any areas that do not receive microwave energy initially are brought to a better cooking position before the cooking process continues.

Microwave cooking is a fast, moist cooking method, ideal for vegetables, fish, rice, sauces, soups, certain meat dishes and poultry. Because of the speed of cooking, tough cuts of meat do not cook successfully. The moist characteristic of this cooking method does not give a crust, so any foods that rely on the formation of a crust for successful cooking cannot be cooked by microwaves alone. Choux pastry, soufflés and batters are examples of recipes that cannot be cooked successfully by microwaves alone.

Cooking Utensils

When using microwaves only do not use metal cooking containers. Avoid any dishes that have metal trims, metal clips and ties or any metal utensils. The exceptions to the no-metal rule when cooking in the microwave only mode are small pieces of cooking foil, used to shield small areas of food that are in danger of overcooking. In some cases, it is possible to use small foil containers (for example, containers for convenience foods) when the majority of the foil area is covered by food. The rule to remember is *follow the manufacturer's instructions*.

Use ovenproof glassware, specially produced plastics and ovenproof china. Most household china is suitable for microwave cooking, some earthenware is useful (although it may absorb a certain amount of microwave energy) and basketware can be used for short-term heating using microwaves only.

Cover food during cooking if it is likely to dry out – use a lid, a plate or special microwave cling film. *Do not use ordinary plastic film*. Roasting bags are suitable for use in the microwave oven – but don't forget to avoid metal ties.

Turn to page 107 for recipes that are cooked by microwaves only. Remember, you can do no harm by slightly undercooking food in the microwave, then putting it back for a few seconds (or minutes) longer but you can ruin food by overcooking it. So, until you are thoroughly familiar with your own oven, keep an eye on what's cooking and if the food looks as though it's ready then open the door – the microwave energy will automatically stop – and take the dish out to check.

Convection Cooking

The great advantage of the combination cooker is that you can use it on the convection mode to cook all your own favourite recipes. Convection cooking uses conventional heat that is recirculated in the oven by means of a fan. The movement of the hot air within the oven cavity speeds up the cooking process. The air moves around the food, rapidly displacing the cold air from the uncooked food. The result is not only speedy cooking, but even heat distribution (and cooking) throughout the oven.

The effect of cooking in a fan-assisted oven is equivalent to about 20 C hotter than the actual setting selected. So, if you put something in to cook at 180 C, because of the recirculated air, the cooking time is equivalent to that required at 200 C in a normal oven. If you are cooking something that requires slow cooking, then reduce the setting accordingly; otherwise reduce the cooking time.

If you make soufflés, then you will find that they are best cooked by convection alone, not on combination mode. There are recipes for soufflés cooked on combination; however, even though they are browned and slightly crisp, they do not give the expected rise and are not, strictly speaking, successful. So stick to conventional heat for cooking soufflés!

Choux pastry is another item that is best cooked by convection alone. I tested a gougère (a ring of choux pastry filled with a mixture of bacon, onion, cheese and other savoury ingredients) and the result was just acceptable. If you put choux pastry in to cook on combination you will find that the microwaves cause it to puff up rapidly, then it sinks slightly as the microwave energy pulses off. Even though the conventional heat works hard at browning the pastry, the crust does not form quickly enough to hold a good rise. The result is not disastrous but it is not good enough to include in the combination recipes. So stick to the method you know already.

Grilling

If your combination oven is fitted with a grill, then use it as you would any ordinary grill. Remember that it can be used in combination with microwaves for very speedy cooking. See pages 13–14 for guidance on combination grilling.

Combination Cookers – Features Available

There are two sizes of combination cookers: the work-top, plug-in oven that is about the same size as the standard microwave oven, or a full-size built-in combination cooker. The majority of the full-size models are significantly more expensive than the table-top ovens.

Controls The controls can be electronic (touch control) or a push button and dial type. The majority of ovens have electronic controls.

In most cases, the temperature and microwave setting are selected, then the cooking time is selected (the order in which these selections are made varies according to the ovens), then the start or cook control is activated. When the cooking time is complete a bell or bleeper will sound. In some cases the noise will continue until you go to the oven and open the door; other models remind you for a short period, then at intervals until the door is opened.

To use some ovens you have to select the microwave setting, microwave cooking time, oven temperature and oven cooking time, then press the start control. The advantage of this type of control system is that you can select a short period of microwave cooking with a longer period of convection cooking and the convection cooking will automatically continue after the microwave cooking time is complete. The disadvantage of this control system is that the process of selection is fairly lengthy and it is possible to forget to give a cooking time for one part of the cooking operation.

Pre-programmed Roasting Some ovens offer a facility for roasting meat or poultry on a pre-programmed setting. In this case you select the roasting function, set the weight of the joint to be cooked and press the start control. The cooking operation has been thoroughly tested by the manufacturer to offer the best possible combination of microwave energy and temperature for roasting the meat. Over the whole of the cooking period the amount of microwave energy and temperature within the oven varies so that the food is cooked to perfection.

Some ovens offer a similar facility for cooking bread, cake, fruit pie, quiche, casseroles and biscuits. The same technique is also available for defrosting certain foods in some ovens.

Certain ovens only offer a number of cooking categories in the combination mode and in each case a particular temperature is combined with a pre-set microwave setting. This type of cooking mode is discussed on page 13.

Preheat Setting Some ovens offer a preheat control. In this case you select the required oven temperature and the preheat function, then press the start control and the oven will automatically preheat. It will bleep when ready. If you want to preheat without this control (if the facility is not available) then select the temperature and the convection cooking mode, then heat for 10 minutes.

Dual Cooking Control or Two Level Cooking In some ovens, if you want to use the rack for two-level cooking, then you have to select this control and the required temperature to ensure even cooking on both levels.

Combination Setting In some cases you have to select the combination cooking function by pressing a certain control before you decide on the microwave setting and the cooking temperature.
Note In some ovens the dual cook term is used for the combination cooking mode and not two-level cooking.

Sensor Cook Some ovens can be programmed to cook food automatically by the amount of moisture released into the oven cavity.

Combination Grilling Some models have a built-in

grill and there can be a control to select the combination grilling mode.

Halogen Heat An alternative to the convection heat and microwave combination is provided by the use of microwave energy with halogen heat. In this case, heat is provided by halogen filaments located in the top and one side of the oven. The microwave energy can be used in combination with the top halogen element or with both top and side elements.

There are five settings that can be selected:
1 Microwaves with top and side halogen heat for roasting and all-round browning.
2 Microwaves with top halogen heat for top browning.
3 Microwaves only.
4 Top halogen heat only for grilling.
5 Top and side halogen heat.

Accessories and their Uses

Most of the work-top combination ovens have turntables. Unlike the standard microwave oven, the combination models come with wire cooking racks. The introduction of metal in the form of a rack into the cooking cavity tends to confuse most people and I cannot offer any scientifically sound explanation for the avoidance or use of metal within a microwave oven!

In addition to a metal rack, a few other accessories come with the oven. The following notes may be of some help in deciding when to use the accessories; remember to read the manufacturer's instructions and follow them closely.

Turntable This can be made of ceramic or metal and it must be in position in order to operate the oven on any cooking mode. In some ovens, the turntable can be stopped when the oven is operated on the convection only setting. This turntable can also be used as a drip pan for roasting.

Splash Guard or Anti-splash Tray This is a perforated metal tray that fits into the turntable, standing slightly above it. When the turntable is used as a drip tray for roasting this splash guard helps to prevent the fat that collects from spitting out during cooking. This tray can be left permanently in position during all cooking operations.

Glass Tray or Drip Tray In ovens that do not have a turntable, there may be a glass tray that slides into the oven. This can be used as a drip tray for roasting or as a shelf for microwave or combination cooking. In other models, a drip tray is provided in addition to the turntable.

ACCESSORIES

Turntable

Splash Guard

Glass Tray or Drip Tray (round)

Glass Tray or Drip Tray (oblong)

Low Rack

High Rack

Insulating Mat

Baking Tray (round)

Baking Tray (oblong)

Handle

Wire Racks All combination ovens come with at least one wire rack. This wire rack should be used for combination cooking and for cooking on the convection mode to allow the free flow of hot air beneath the food. In some cases, where two items are to be cooked at once, food in the cooking dish can be placed straight on the turntable, with the second item positioned on the wire rack above. The position of the dishes is usually swopped over during cooking.

In ovens that do not have a turntable, the wire rack slides in as in a normal, full-sized oven. This rack can be used for all cooking modes.

Some models provide a high rack and a low rack. These can be used together for two-level convection cooking (follow the instructions with the oven) and the high one can be used for grilling, where the food should be positioned near the top of the oven.

Insulating Mat This accessory is provided with some ovens. It is usually covered with a non-stick coating. It is placed between the wire rack and metal baking tins when cooking using the combination mode. This mat prevents any sparking between the metal of the rack and the baking tin (see cooking utensils for comments on the use of metal). This insulating mat can also be used as a base for cooking certain pastry items like apple turnovers or Cornish pasties. If the food holds its shape well, then it can be placed straight on the insulating mat and it will receive the maximum possible hot air from the base to give best cooking results. The non-stick coating makes for easy cleaning.

Baking Tray Some ovens come with a circular tray to fit on the turntable, or with an oblong tray that slides into the oven if there is no turntable. This can be used for cooking individual food items or for making pizza and similar items.

Handle Some manufacturers supply a heavy, detachable metal handle which is useful for lifting the circular tray out of an oven that has a turntable. This is particularly useful when food is being cooked under the grill.

Cooking Utensils

The same boring old rule applies here as with all other aspects of cooking in microwave ovens – follow the manufacturer's instructions when it comes to selecting cooking utensils. The following notes are a guide, you will probably find that you have plenty of suitable cookware in the kitchen, so it is not a good idea to rush out and spend a fortune on specialist cookware.

Metal Some manufacturers recommend the use of metal on combination cooking mode. Do not use metal baking tins if cooking with microwaves only. In some ovens if you use metal tins when cooking with microwaves and convection mode, then remember to use the insulating mat provided. You can safely and effectively use metal tins when cooking on the convection mode only.

Throughout the recipes, I recommend the use of a dish instead of a baking tin when using the combination mode. The reason for this is simple: the microwaves do not pass through metal, therefore the food does not receive any microwave energy through the sides or base of a tin, just from the top. This lack of microwave energy can result in an inferior result or lengthy cooking times in some cases. For this reason cooking dishes (made of ovenproof glass, or ceramic) give a better result whenever microwaves are used.

When cooking shallow items, you will find that a dish that allows the microwaves to pass through from the base as well as the sides can give a better result than a tin. So the above comment is true even if the cake or food item is a shallow one.

Ovenproof Glassware and Ceramic Dishes These are ideal for use in the combination oven. Avoid any with metal trims or decorations as they will cause sparking. Remember the combination oven gets very hot so the dishes must withstand the heat.

Specially Manufactured Plastics There are certain ranges of plastic cookware designed for use in microwave ovens and up to temperatures of 200 C. From testing, I found that many of the recipes cooked quickly and best at temperatures above 200 C. This type of cookware is very expensive and, of course, it is re-useable. However, it does not stand up to really heavy wear over long periods of time. Cake dishes, unusual shaped dishes and items that are not going to be worked to death are good value. For day-to-day cooking for main meals you are probably better off with ovenproof china or sturdy ovenproof glassware.

Roasting Bags These are useful to prevent splattering and they can also be used for microwave only cooking.

When Using Microwaves Only Avoid all metal, other than very shallow foil containers used for convenience foods and small pieces of cooking foil used to prevent small areas of food from overcooking.

Use heatproof china and plastics that withstand heat. Use basins, ovenproof glass measuring jugs, mixing bowls, flan dishes and casseroles. Dinner plates are also useful. Absorbent kitchen paper can be used for baking potatoes or to cover foods that may splatter.

Specialist microwave ware is, of course, perfectly safe and ideal for cooking a wide variety of foods. Take stock of your existing kitchen equipment before spending money on unnecessary specialist items.

Baskets and wood are suitable for short-term heating. Earthenware absorbs some microwave energy but is still useful for all methods of cooking in the combination oven.

Pre-programmed Settings

Some ovens do not allow you to select the temperature and microwave setting when using the combination mode. Instead they provide numbered settings each of which combines a certain microwave input with a particular temperature. For example:

Setting	Microwave Input	Temperature
1	Low	160 C
2	Low	180 C
3	Medium-low	180 C
4	Medium-low	200 C

The above settings are only examples – the instructions book will tell you exactly what the settings are on your oven if it is pre-programmed. Alternatively the manufacturer may provide all the details you need to know which setting to use for a variety of cooking processes without spelling out the precise combinations of temperature and microwave power settings.

For example:

Setting	Suggested uses	Setting	Suggested uses
C1	Rich fruit cakes and light pâtés		foods (e.g. Cornish pasties), syrup or bakewell tarts or similar shortcrust pastries
C2	Roasting large turkeys or goose, casseroling tougher cuts of meat	C6	Roasting meat and poultry (except large birds), large scones or pizza bases, vegetable casseroles, puff pastry, bread
C3	Semi-rich fruit cakes, heavy pâtés, steak and kidney stew, lightly cooked fish		
C4	Braising steak, pork chops or tender casseroles, cooking whole salmon or gingerbread	C7	Chicken casseroles, small whole fish e.g. trout
C5	Lamb hotpots, mince dishes, pastry-wrapped uncooked	C8	Roast chicken portions
		C9	Combination grilling

To follow the recipes in this book, select the setting that offers the combination nearest to the microwave setting and oven temperature stated in the recipe. You may find that the setting you use has a lower microwave input and slightly cooler oven, in which case you will have to increase the overall cooking time. Remember, it is best to slightly undercook the food, then put it back for a few minutes, than overcook it. If you are unable to select the temperature/microwave setting nearest to the combination given in the recipes, then follow the manufacturer's guidance for using the settings. For example select a setting suggested for baking bread, cakes or pastry; or a setting used for roasting.

The combination cooking mode is the same even if you vary the power inputs and temperature, so you should find that these recipes work well in a pre-programmed oven even if the timing is slightly different. When you do cook a recipe, note the setting and cooking time next to the method for future reference.

Combination Grilling

If your appliance offers the facility for grilling in combination with microwave cooking, then maximise the use of it by cooking small cuts of meat or poultry in this way. The following chart outlines some basic cooking methods.

Combination Grilling Small Cuts of Poultry

Use grill on hottest setting

	Microwave Power Setting	Cooking Time in Minutes	Cooking Instructions
Chicken Quarters	High		Place in dish, skin down, turn halfway through cooking.
–2.		8–10	
–4		12–15	As above.
Boneless Chicken Breasts	High		As above.
–2		5–6	
–4		10–12	
Drumsticks			Arrange drumsticks with thick parts towards outside of dish. Turn over halfway through cooking.
–4	High	7–8	
–8	High	11–14	
Duck Quarters			Place portions, skin down in dish, then turn over halfway through cooking.
–2	High	12–15	
–4	High	20–22	

Combination Grilling Small Cuts of Meat

Steak			
2 (225-g/8-oz)			Brush with a little oil or melted butter, then turn over halfway through cooking.
–medium	Medium	5–7	
–well done	Medium	8–9	
4 (225-g/8-oz)			
–medium	Medium	10–11	
–well done	Medium	12–13	
Lamb Chops			Place in dish, brush with a little oil and turn over halfway through cooking.
–2	Medium	8–10	
–4	Medium	10–12	
Pork Chops			As above.
–2	Medium	10–12	
–4	Medium	14–17	

Combination Grilling continued

Microwave energy combined with the use of a hot grill cooks food very fast and is not suitable for baking cakes or bread, or for roasting joints of meat. Combination grilling can be used for whole fish (mackerel, sardines and trout for example), for poultry (whole chickens, chicken portions, duck or turkey portions), for steaks, chops or sausages, for gratins and made-up dishes (such as cottage pie or lasagne).

Throughout the chapters you will find notes on certain recipes that are suitable for combination grilling. Because the grill browns and crisps the food quickly, a high microwave setting can be used to cook the food at a similarly fast rate.

Even though the charts give you some idea of the cooking times remember that as with all grilling you do have to keep a close watch on the food as it cooks and use your judgement as to when cooking is complete.

Cooking a Complete Meal

My first attempt at cooking a traditional roast dinner in the combination microwave oven was not altogether successful – I confidently entrusted the Sunday roast to the shiny cavity of the bright new appliance and extolled the virtues of this speedy cooking method to my fascinated mother. The apple pie had already cooked to perfection, the roast turned out equally well, then I cooked the vegetables and realised my mistake. The runner beans and peas cooked well by microwaves but the heat remaining in the oven did not give a good result!

You can cook a complete meal in the combination microwave oven with great success but do stop and think before you start cooking. Following the episode with the half-baked runner beans and peas I follow these guidelines.

1 Prepare vegetables and sauces cooked by microwaves only in advance, leaving them slightly undercooked so that they can be heated quickly just before serving.

2 Prepare any other recipes that are cooked by microwaves only – for example, a starter or pudding, remembering to slightly undercook if you are going to reheat the dish later.

3 Prepare any dessert that is suitable for cooking in advance and that requires the combination cooking mode.

4 Cook the main dish and make the gravy or any sauce based on the meat juices.

5 Quickly heat the vegetables on microwaves only and serve.

By following these guidelines you should produce a meal that is ready in the right order. The vegetables should be heated for just one or two minutes before serving so that they do not have time to dry out in the residual heat from combination cooking. The main point to emphasise is to avoid cooking by microwaves only in a hot oven if you are cooking food that benefits from a moist cooking method.

Care of the Oven

One comment that is frequently made about combination microwave cookers is that they are difficult to clean because of the baked-on effect of microwaves and heat. I really did not experience a problem in keeping the oven clean – even when testing several roast joints.

Wipe the oven out frequently to remove any splattering or bits of food before they have time to bake on to the surface. Always follow the manufacturer's instructions when it comes to the cleaning materials to use.

When cooking foods that are likely to spit and splatter, and if it is possible, then cover the dish. When roasting meats or grilling cuts of meat, I find that they produce less mess if cooked in a shallow dish – a quiche dish is ideal. If you do use the rack, then always use the splatter guard provided in the turntable.

It is vitally important to keep the door, its surround and all areas near the opening very clean. Remove the turntable and other items that can be washed (like the cooking racks) and wash them frequently to avoid any build up of baked-on deposits.

Top Leek Soup Surprise (page 16)
Bottom Ham Soufflé in Artichokes (page 17)

·FIRST·
COURSES

FRENCH ONION SOUP

 HIGH

Combination:

 HIGH/MEDIUM

◆ 250 C

SERVES 4

450 g/1 lb onions, sliced and separated into rings
knob of butter
1.15 litres/2 pints good beef stock

salt and freshly ground black pepper
4 tablespoons dry sherry
4 thick slices French bread
75 g/3 oz Emmental cheese, grated

Put the onions in a large casserole dish with a knob of butter. Pour in the stock and add seasoning to taste. Cover and cook using microwaves only on high for 15–18 minutes, or until the soup is boiling and the onions are cooked. Stir well, taste and adjust the seasoning, then add the sherry. Heat the oven to 250 C.

When the oven is hot, float the bread in the soup and sprinkle with the cheese. Bake at 250 C using medium microwave setting for 3–5 minutes, or until the cheese is lightly browned. Serve immediately.

LEEK SOUP SURPRISE

 HIGH

Combination:

 MEDIUM

 250 C

SERVES 4

Illustrated on page 15

◆ These satisfying soup pots make a delicious, warming lunch or supper dish. Use the same idea for other soups if you like.

350 g/12 oz leeks, sliced
350 g/12 oz potatoes, cubed
25 g/1 oz butter
2 tablespoons plain flour
450 ml/$\frac{3}{4}$ pint chicken stock

salt and freshly ground black pepper
150 ml/$\frac{1}{4}$ pint milk or single cream
1 (250-g/8$\frac{3}{4}$-oz) packet puff pastry, defrosted if frozen
beaten egg to glaze

Put the leeks in a colander and wash them thoroughly, separating the rings and rinsing out any grit. Shake off the excess water, then put the leeks in a large casserole dish or mixing bowl. Add the potatoes and butter. Cover and cook using microwaves only on high for 5 minutes.

Stir in the flour, then gradually pour in the stock, stirring all the time. Add a little seasoning and continue to cook in the microwave on high for 15–18 minutes, or until the vegetables are tender and the soup is cooked. Stir in the milk or cream and taste, adding extra seasoning if necessary. Leave to cool.

Heat the oven to 250 C. Ladle the soup into four individual casserole dishes or ovenproof bowls that are not too wide across the top. Cut the pastry into quarters. Roll out each portion into a circle large enough to cover one of the bowls. From any pastry trimmings cut shapes to decorate the pastry lids. Brush the shapes with a little beaten egg and press them on to the middle of the pastry circles. (Once the pastry tops are lifted over the soup they need careful handling to avoid pushing them into the dishes, so this is the stage at which to add the decoration.) Brush the edges of the dishes with a little beaten egg and lift a pastry circle over each one. Press the edge of the pastry firmly on to the rims of the dishes, taking care not to press the middle down on to the soup. Brush the tops very lightly with beaten egg.

Bake at 250 C and medium microwave setting for 7–8 minutes, or until the pastry is well puffed and browned. Serve at once.

SOUFFLÉD AVOCADOS

Combination:

 MEDIUM

 250 C

SERVES 4

40 g/1½ oz Cheddar cheese, grated
1 tablespoon grated Parmesan cheese
1 teaspoon prepared mustard
1 tablespoon snipped chives
1 tablespoon plain flour

salt and freshly ground black pepper
1 tablespoon milk
1 large egg, separated
2 ripe avocados
a little lemon juice

Heat the oven to 250 C. Mix the cheeses, mustard, chives, flour and seasoning in a basin. Beat in the milk and egg yolk.

Cut the avocados in half and remove the stones. Sprinkle with a little lemon juice to prevent discoloration. Place the avocado halves on a flan dish, using pieces of crumpled greaseproof paper to support them on the level.

Whisk the egg white until stiff, then use a metal spoon to fold it into the cheese mixture. Spoon the cheese mixture into the avocados and bake immediately at 250 C using medium microwave setting for 5 minutes, or until the soufflé filling has risen and browned. Serve at once. Crisp toast is a good accompaniment for this starter.

HAM SOUFFLÉ IN ARTICHOKES

 HIGH

Combination:

 MEDIUM

220 C

SERVES 4

Illustrated on page 15

4 globe artichokes
225 g/8 oz cooked ham, minced or finely chopped
3 tablespoons plain flour

salt and freshly ground black pepper
2 tablespoons chopped chives
1 tablespoon milk
2 eggs, separated

Cut off and discard the artichoke stalks, wash the artichokes thoroughly and place in a large roasting bag. Cook using microwaves only on high for about 20 minutes, or until one of the base leaves comes off easily. Leave until cool enough to handle. Trim off the leaf tips, pull out the centre leaves, then use a small teaspoon to tease the hairy choke off the artichoke base in one neat piece. Make sure any stray hairs are removed. Heat the oven to 220 C.

Mix the ham, flour, a little seasoning and the chives, then stir in the milk and egg yolks. Whisk the whites until they are stiff, then use a metal spoon to fold them into the ham mixture. Stand the artichokes on a flan dish and fill with the ham mixture. Bake at 220 C using medium microwave setting for 8–10 minutes, or until well risen and browned. Serve immediately with thin bread and butter or melba toast.

SAVOURY MUSHROOMS

 HIGH

Combination:

 MEDIUM

◆ 250 C

SERVES 4

1 small onion, finely chopped
2 cloves garlic, crushed
knob of butter
4 large open mushrooms
100 g/4 oz fresh breadcrumbs

2 tomatoes, peeled and chopped
salt and freshly ground black pepper
2 tablespoons chopped parsley
3–4 tablespoons milk
25 g/1 oz butter

Put the onion and garlic in a basin with the butter and cook using microwaves only on high for 3 minutes. Heat the oven to 250 C.

Cut the stalks off the mushrooms. Put the wiped caps in a greased dish – a flan dish is suitable, as is any other large flat dish which will hold the mushrooms and fit in the oven. Finely chop the stalks and mix them with the onion and garlic. Add the breadcrumbs, tomato, seasoning and parsley. Stir in enough milk to bind the mixture.

Divide the filling between the mushroom caps, pressing it into them and piling up the filling. Top each with a little butter and bake at 250 C using medium microwave setting for 5–7 minutes. Serve freshly cooked.

ONION TARTS

 HIGH

Combination:

 MEDIUM

◆ 250 C

SERVES 4

◆ These delicious onion tarts are light and well flavoured. For a first course fold in the egg whites and bake just 5 minutes before serving.

Pastry
75 g/3 oz plain flour
40 g/1½ oz margarine
1 tablespoon water
Filling
350 g/12 oz onions, finely chopped

knob of butter
1 tablespoon plain flour
2 eggs, separated
salt and freshly ground black pepper
2 tablespoons chopped parsley

Put the flour in a bowl, then rub in the margarine until the mixture resembles fine breadcrumbs. Add just enough water to bind the ingredients together then mix with the fingertips. Cut the pastry into quarters. Roll out each piece into a circle large enough to line a 7.5-cm/3-in flan dish. Press the pastry circles into the dishes, trim the edges and prick the bases. Chill.

Put the onions in a large basin with the butter and cook using microwaves only on high for 5 minutes. Heat the oven to 250 C. Stir the flour into the onions, then stir in the egg yolks, seasoning and the parsley.

Cook the pastry cases at 250 C using medium microwave setting for 5 minutes. Whisk the egg whites until stiff, then stir a little into the onion mixture. Use a metal spoon to fold the rest of the egg white into the mixture. Divide the filling between the pastry shells, piling it up neatly. Bake at 250 C using medium microwave setting for 4–5 minutes, or until lightly browned. Serve immediately.

Top Bacon-wrapped Trout (page 20)
Bottom Captain's Cobbler (page 21)

FISH DISHES

PARCELLED COD STEAKS

Combination:

 MEDIUM

◆ 250 C

SERVES 4

◆ A good way of turning two thick cod steaks into a meal for four. To add an elaborate pastry decoration, use a 370-g/ 13-oz packet of pastry and roll it out slightly larger. Cut out leaves or thin strips to top the parcels.

2 (350-g/12-oz) cod steaks
100 g/4 oz button mushrooms, chopped
2 tomatoes, peeled and chopped
salt and freshly ground black pepper
1 teaspoon dill weed
1 (250-g/8¾-oz) packet puff pastry, defrosted if frozen
1 egg, beaten

Using a sharp, pointed knife, remove the skin from the cod steaks. Carefully cut the fish off the central bones to give four thick, almost round, portions. Fold any flap of fish round the steak to neaten the shape if necessary.

Mix the mushroom with the tomato. Add a little seasoning and the dill. Heat the oven to 250 C.

On a lightly floured surface, roll out the pastry into a 35.5-cm/14-in square. Cut the pastry into four equal pieces. Divide the mushroom mixture between the squares and place a portion of fish on top of each. Brush the edges of the pastry with a little beaten egg, then fold them over to enclose the fish completely.

Put the parcels on a large flan dish (or any large flat dish that fits into the oven), placing the pastry joins underneath. Using the point of a knife, lightly score a criss-cross pattern on top of the pastry, taking care not to cut right through it. Brush with a little beaten egg and bake at 250 C using medium microwave setting for 15 minutes, or until the pastry is well puffed and golden. Serve freshly cooked.

COULIBIAC

 HIGH

Combination:

 MEDIUM

 250 C

SERVES 4–6

◆ This Russian fish pie combines cooked rice with salmon and vegetables to make a substantial meal. Serve with soured cream if you like.

1 small onion, finely chopped
75 g/3 oz long-grain rice
300 ml/½ pint boiling water
2 tablespoons chopped parsley
2 hard-boiled eggs, chopped
225 g/8 oz smoked salmon offcuts
100 g/4 oz French beans, cooked and cut up
1 (370-g/13-oz) packet puff pastry, defrosted if frozen
1 egg, beaten

Put the onion, rice and water in a large basin, cover with a plate or microwave cling film and cook using microwaves only on high for 10 minutes. Leave to cool. Heat the oven to 250 C. Stir all the remaining ingredients except the pastry and beaten egg into the rice.

Cut the pastry in half. On a lightly floured surface roll out each piece of pastry into an 18 × 25-cm/7 × 10-in oval. Pile the rice mixture up in the middle of one piece and brush the pastry edges with a little beaten egg. When you mound the rice mixture on the pastry you will have to press it into a neat pile. Lift the second piece of pastry over the top and press the edges together to seal in the filling.

Using a pair of kitchen scissors, make short snips into the pastry all over the top of the coulibiac. Lift on to a large flan dish and pinch the edges to give a decorative finish. Brush with beaten egg and bake at 250 C using medium microwave setting for 8–10 minutes, or until the pastry is well puffed and browned. Serve hot or cold, with soured cream spooned on to individual portions. A light tomato and onion salad is an excellent accompaniment for this dish.

CAPTAIN'S COBBLER

 HIGH

Combination:

 MEDIUM

 250 C

SERVES 4

Illustrated on page 19

1 large leek, sliced
2 large carrots, sliced
knob of butter or a little oil
2 tablespoons plain flour
450 ml/¾ pint fish stock
bay leaf
salt and freshly ground black pepper
450 g/1 lb white fish fillet, skinned and cut
   into chunks (cod, haddock or coley)

2 tablespoons chopped parsley
Cobbler Topping
225 g/8 oz self-raising flour
50 g/2 oz butter or margarine
3 teaspoons baking powder
1 teaspoon dried mixed herbs
50 g/2 oz cheese, grated
1 egg, beaten
about 5 tablespoons milk, plus extra to glaze

Thoroughly wash the leek, separating the slices into rings to make sure that all grit is removed. Mix the leek with the carrot and the knob of butter or oil in a casserole dish. Select a deep dish so that there is plenty of room for the other ingredients and for the cobbler topping. Cook using microwaves only on high for 5 minutes. Stir in the flour, then gradually pour in the stock, stirring all the time. Add the bay leaf and a little seasoning. Cook on high for a further 5–7 minutes, or until the stock is almost boiling. Add the fish and parsley to the casserole and mix well, taking care not to break up the fish. Heat the oven to 250 C.

For the topping, put the flour in a bowl and rub in the fat. Add the baking powder, herbs and cheese and mix well. Stir in the beaten egg and enough milk to make a soft scone dough. Turn the dough out on to a lightly floured surface and knead it very lightly until just smooth. Cut the dough into eight equal portions and roll each one into a ball, then flatten slightly to make a thick domed scone. Without overlapping them, arrange the scones on top of the fish, round the edge of the dish. Brush with a little milk.

Bake at 250 C using medium microwave setting for about 10 minutes, or until the cobblers are risen and browned. Serve freshly cooked. You may like to offer an additional green vegetable (peas or French beans, for example) with the cobbler, but the topping is quite filling and will replace potatoes, pasta or rice.

BACON-WRAPPED TROUT

Combination:

 MEDIUM

 250 C

SERVES 4

Illustrated on page 19

4 trout, cleaned with heads on
4 bay leaves
4 parsley sprigs
4 strips of lemon rind

4 rindless rashers smoked bacon
Garnish
lemon wedges
fresh bay leaves or parsley sprigs

Heat the oven to 250 C. Trim the fins off the trout. Place a bay leaf, parsley sprig and strip of lemon rind in each fish. Wrap a rasher of bacon around each trout, then place in two flan dishes.

Put one dish on the turntable and the second on the rack above. Cook at 250 C using medium microwave setting for 6 minutes. Swop the positions of the dishes, then continue to cook for a further 4 minutes. Serve immediately, garnished with lemon wedges and bay leaves or parsley sprigs.

FISH PIE

 HIGH

Combination:

 MEDIUM

 220 C

SERVES 4

1 onion, chopped
25 g/1 oz butter
2 tablespoons plain flour
300 ml/½ pint milk
salt and freshly ground black pepper
75 g/3 oz Cheddar cheese, grated

350 g/12 oz white fish fillet, skinned and cut
   into chunks (cod, coley or haddock)
2 tablespoons chopped parsley
1 (250-g/8¾-oz) packet puff pastry,
   defrosted if frozen
beaten egg to glaze

Put the onion and butter in a pie dish. Cook using microwaves only on high for 3 minutes. Stir in the flour, then gradually pour in the milk, stirring all the time. Add a little seasoning and cook on high for a further 3 minutes. Whisk the sauce thoroughly. Heat the oven to 220 C. Add the cheese to the sauce and stir well. Mix in the fish, taking care not to break up the pieces. Lastly add the parsley.

Roll out the pastry on a lightly floured surface into a piece large enough to cover the top of the pie with about 5 cm/2 in extra. Cut a narrow strip from the edge of the pastry. Dampen the rim of the dish and press the pastry strip on to it. Brush the pastry strip with a little water. Lift the pastry lid over the pie and press the pastry edges together firmly. Trim off any excess and use the blunt side of a knife to tap the edge of the pastry, at the same time pressing down firmly on top of the pastry to push the edge outwards. This process, known as *knocking up*, seals the pastry to prevent the filling leaking during cooking. Neaten the pie by marking scallops round the edge. If you like, roll out the pastry trimmings and cut out decorative shapes to put on top of the pie.

Glaze the pastry with a little beaten egg and bake in the oven at 220 C using medium microwave setting for 10 minutes, or until the pastry is well puffed and golden. Serve freshly cooked.

ALTERNATIVE METHOD
The pie can be cooked at 220 C using low microwave setting for about 20 minutes. Take care not to over-brown the top, turning off the conventional heat for the last few minutes if necessary.

VARIATIONS
The above is a straightforward recipe for a plain fish pie and it can be varied by adding colourful or full-flavoured ingredients to the filling.
Special Seafood Pie Substitute 150 ml/¼ pint fish stock and 150 ml/¼ pint dry white wine for the milk. Omit the cheese. Use 225 g/8 oz halibut or cod and add 100 g/4 oz peeled cooked prawns (defrosted if frozen), 100 g/4 oz shelled cooked mussels (use the cooking liquor as part of the measured stock for the sauce) and 1 teaspoon grated lemon rind. This dish is excellent for dinner parties, particularly when served with cooked asparagus, mange-tout peas or broccoli. New potatoes, when in season, are an excellent accompaniment.
Smoked Fish Pie Reduce the quantity of cheese to 50 g/2 oz and substitute smoked haddock, cod or coley for the white fish. Add the grated rind of half a lemon.

Top Duck with Orange and Tarragon Sauce (page 33)
Bottom Mexican-style Turkey Fillets (page 29)

· POULTRY · AND GAME

POULTRY AND GAME ROASTING CHART

	MICROWAVE POWER SETTING	TEMPERATURE °C	TIME IN MINUTES PER 450 G/1 LB	COOKING INSTRUCTIONS
Chicken, whole	Medium	220	7–9	Preheat oven. Put chicken in dish and dot with a little fat or brush with oil. Turn over twice, ending with breast side uppermost.
Chicken quarters –2	Medium	240–250	Total cooking time: 10–12 minutes	Preheat oven. Turn joints once, starting skin side down and ending with skin uppermost.
Chicken quarters –4	Medium	240–250	Total cooking time: 15–16 minutes	As above
Turkey	Medium	200	6–7	Do not preheat oven. Place turkey in dish. Turn twice, baste several times. Leave to stand 15 minutes before serving.
Duck	Medium	240–250	7–8	Preheat oven. Place duck in dish. Prick skin all over and rub with a little salt. Turn twice, draining off excess fat. Stand 5 minutes before serving.
Duck joints –2	High	240–250	5	As above
	Medium	240–250	Total cooking time: 10–12 minutes	Prick skin, rub with salt. Turn twice, ending with skin side uppermost.
Duck joints –4	Medium	240–250	Total cooking time: 25–30 minutes	As above
Pheasant –2	Medium	220–240	Total cooking time: 18–20 minutes	Preheat oven. Place in dish, breast side up. Place halved bacon rasher on top. Turn over twice, ending breast side up and remove bacon to brown.
Pheasant –4	Medium	220–240	Total cooking time: 25 minutes	As above

STUFFINGS FOR ROAST POULTRY

Sage and Onion Finely chop 1 large onion and place in a basin with a knob of butter. Cook using microwaves only on high for 3 minutes. Mix with 225 g/8 oz fresh breadcrumbs, 1 tablespoon finely chopped fresh sage or rubbed sage, plenty of seasoning and enough milk to bind the ingredients.

Parsley and Thyme Make the stuffing as above, substituting 4 tablespoons chopped fresh parsley and 1 tablespoon chopped fresh or dried thyme for the sage.

Fresh Herb and Walnut Prepare the stuffing as for sage and onion, using 175 g/6 oz fresh breadcrumbs and 2 tablespoons chopped fresh herbs. Add 100 g/4 oz finely chopped walnuts before mixing in the milk.

ROAST CHICKEN WITH SPICY RICE STUFFING

 HIGH

Combination:

 MEDIUM

 220 C

SERVES 4

◆ Take this recipe as a guide to cooking any roast stuffed chicken. Alternative stuffings are given on page 24.

1 onion, chopped
¼ teaspoon turmeric
1 teaspoon ground coriander
1 teaspoon cinnamon
75 g/3 oz long-grain rice
175 ml/6 fl oz water
25 g/1 oz sultanas

175 g/6 oz dessert apples, peeled, cored and chopped
salt and freshly ground black pepper
1 (1.5-kg/3½-lb) oven-ready chicken
25 g/1 oz butter
1 clove garlic, crushed
grated rind of ½ lemon

Put the onion in a basin with the spices, rice and water. Cover and cook using microwaves only on high for 10 minutes. Heat the oven to 220 C. Add the sultanas, apples and seasoning to the rice, then use a spoon to press the stuffing into the body cavity of the chicken. Cream the butter with the garlic and lemon rind. Spread this mixture all over the top of the chicken.

Place the chicken in a large flan dish and roast at 220 C using medium microwave setting for 25–30 minutes, or until the chicken is cooked and browned. To check that the bird is cooked, pierce the meat at the thickest part of the body, near the thigh joints. The juices should be free of blood.

ALTERNATIVE METHOD
The chicken can be cooked at 220 C using low microwave setting for about 35–40 minutes.

GALANTINE OF CHICKEN

 HIGH

Combination:

 MEDIUM

 220 C

SERVES 4–6

◆ Follow the same method for boning a chicken as for boning a turkey.

1 small leek, chopped
knob of butter
1 teaspoon rubbed sage
½ teaspoon dried thyme
salt and freshly ground black pepper

175 g/6 oz fresh breadcrumbs
1 red pepper, deseeded and chopped
175 g/6 oz cooked ham, diced
1 (1.5-kg/3½-lb) chicken, boned (see page 30)
knob of butter or a little oil

Put the leek in a basin with the butter and cook using microwaves only on high for 3 minutes. Mix in the herbs, seasoning and half the breadcrumbs. Heat the oven to 220 C.

Mix the remaining breadcrumbs with the red pepper and ham, adding seasoning to taste. Open the chicken out flat on a board. Spread half the ham stuffing on it, then put the leek stuffing on top. Top with the remaining ham mixture. Use a trussing needle or large darning needle and strong thread to sew up the chicken into a neat shape. Place in a large flan dish and dot with butter or brush with oil.

Roast at 220 C using medium microwave setting for 20–25 minutes; turn the chicken over halfway through cooking. Serve hot or cold, sliced.

BAKED CHICKEN KIEV

Combination:

◈ MEDIUM

◆ 250 C

SERVES 4

◆ A very successful way of cooking this well-known recipe – far better than the inconvenience of deep frying.

50 g/2 oz butter
2 cloves garlic, crushed
2 tablespoons chopped parsley
salt and freshly ground black pepper
4 boneless chicken breasts, skinned
1 egg, beaten

2 tablespoons water
100–175 g/4–6 oz fresh white breadcrumbs
Garnish
1 red pepper, deseeded and chopped
¼ cucumber, sliced
1 lemon, cut into wedges

Mix the butter, garlic and parsley. Beat in seasoning, then divide into quarters and form each portion into a small pat. Wrap in cling film and chill thoroughly (this can be done in the freezer for speed).

Make a small slit in the middle of each chicken breast and press in a pat of the butter mixture. Press the meat back together to enclose the butter completely. Beat the egg and water together. Coat each chicken breast in the mixture, then press on a thick coating of breadcrumbs. Repeat to ensure that the coating is thick and even. Chill for at least 15 minutes.

Heat the oven to 250 C. Arrange the chicken on a well greased flan dish. Bake at 250 C using medium microwave setting for 17–20 minutes, or until the coating is well browned. The chicken should be firm and the butter centre will have melted.

Serve immediately, garnished with some chopped red pepper and cucumber slices. Accompany each portion with a couple of lemon wedges so that the juice can be squeezed over as required.

TANDOORI CHICKEN

Combination:

 MEDIUM

 250 C

SERVES 4

4 chicken joints, skinned
1 small onion, grated
5 cloves garlic, crushed
25 g/1 oz fresh root ginger, grated
2 teaspoons ground coriander
1 teaspoon ground cumin
1 teaspoon ground cinnamon
1 teaspoon turmeric

$\frac{1}{2}$ teaspoon salt
$\frac{1}{4}$ teaspoon freshly ground black pepper
150 ml/$\frac{1}{4}$ pint natural yogurt
juice of 1 lemon
Garnish
1 lemon, cut into wedges
1 lettuce heart
1 onion, thinly sliced

Cut three slits in each piece of chicken, then place in a bowl. Mix all the remaining ingredients and pour over the chicken. Cover and leave in the refrigerator for at least 24 hours. This dish is best left to marinate for a couple of days (make sure the chicken is really fresh).

Heat the oven to 250 C. Put the chicken joints in a flan dish and pour over the marinade. Roast at 250 C using medium microwave setting for 10 minutes, turn the joints and continue cooking for a further 5–7 minutes.

Serve garnished with lemon wedges, small lettuce leaves and plenty of onion rings. Pilau rice is a traditional accompaniment (see recipe on page 118).

ALTERNATIVE METHOD
This recipe can be cooked at 250 C using low microwave setting for about 10–12 minutes. If you prefer follow the instructions for combination grilling on page 13.

COQ AU VIN

 HIGH

Combination:

 MEDIUM

 220 C

SERVES 4

◆ For the best results, skin the chicken joints and soak them in the wine overnight before cooking.

1 large onion, chopped
225 g/8 oz rindless streaky bacon, chopped
2 cloves garlic, crushed
25 g/1 oz butter
2 tablespoons plain flour
salt and freshly ground black pepper

bay leaf
450 ml/¾ pint red wine
2 parsley sprigs
2 sprigs of thyme
4 chicken joints, skinned if preferred
1 tablespoon chopped parsley to garnish

Place the onion, bacon and garlic in a large casserole dish with the butter. Cook using microwaves only on high for 3 minutes. Stir in the flour, a generous sprinkling of seasoning and the bay leaf. Pour in the wine, stirring all the time, then add the herbs.

Place the chicken joints in the dish and spoon the sauce over them. Bake at 220 C (no need to preheat the oven; the chicken needs to be slightly browned) using medium microwave setting for 10 minutes. Turn the chicken joints over, basting them with the sauce, then cook for a further 10–15 minutes, or until the chicken is cooked. When the chicken is pierced, the juices should be free of blood.

Serve the casserole, with bay leaf and herb sprigs removed, sprinkled with chopped parsley. Buttered pasta is a good accompaniment and a crisp side salad makes the perfect complement.

CHICKEN AND MUSHROOM PIE

 HIGH

Combination:

 MEDIUM

 250 C

SERVES 4

450 g/1 lb uncooked, boneless chicken meat, diced
100 g/4 oz mushrooms, sliced
knob of butter
salt and freshly ground black pepper
2 tablespoons plain flour
300 ml/½ pint boiling water

bay leaf
2 tablespoons chopped parsley
2 teaspoons chopped fresh or 1 teaspoon dried thyme
1 quantity Shortcrust Pastry (page 68)
1 egg, beaten, to glaze

Mix the chicken with the mushrooms and butter in a pie dish. Cover with a plate or special microwave cling film and cook using microwaves only on high for 6 minutes. Stir well, adding salt and pepper and the flour. Pour in the boiling water, then add the bay leaf and other herbs. Mix well. Heat the oven to 250 C.

Roll out the pastry about 2.5 cm/1 in larger than the top of the pie dish. Trim a narrow strip from the edge of the pastry and dampen the rim of the dish. Press the strip of pastry on to the dish, then brush the pastry edge with a little water. Lift the pastry lid on to the pie, press down the edge firmly to seal in the filling and trim off any excess pastry. Knock up and pinch scallop shapes round the edge. If you like, re-roll the trimmings and cut out decorative shapes to put on top of the pie. Brush a little beaten egg over the pie.

Bake at 250 C using medium microwave setting for 10–15 minutes, or until the top of the pie is cooked and browned and the chicken is cooked through. Serve piping hot.

CHICKEN AND BROCCOLI PIE WITH CREAM CHEESE PASTRY

 HIGH

Combination:

 MEDIUM

 250 C

SERVES 4

1 onion, chopped
450 g/1 lb broccoli, trimmed and chopped
knob of butter
450 g/1 lb uncooked boneless chicken meat, cubed
2 tablespoons plain flour
300 ml/½ pint dry white wine or dry cider
salt and freshly ground black pepper

Cream Cheese Pastry
175 g/6 oz self-raising flour
50 g/2 oz butter
75 g/3 oz cream cheese
salt
1 teaspoon dried marjoram
2 tablespoons water
1 egg, beaten, to glaze

Put the onion, broccoli and butter in a pie dish, cover with a plate or microwave cling film and cook using microwaves only on high for 5 minutes. Add the chicken, stir, re-cover and cook for a further 5 minutes. Heat the oven to 250 C. Stir the flour into the chicken mixture, then add the wine or cider and a generous sprinkling of seasoning.

For the pastry, put the flour in a bowl, then rub in the butter and cream cheese. The mixture will not give as fine a texture as a shortcrust pastry mixture, but the cream cheese should be evenly distributed. Add a pinch of salt and the marjoram. Mix in the water and gather the pastry together with your fingertips.

On a lightly floured surface, roll out the pastry into a piece large enough to cover the top of the pie with about 2.5 cm/1 in to spare. Cut a narrow strip and press it on to the dampened rim of the dish. Dampen the pastry edge with a little water. Lift the pastry lid over the pie, pressing the edges well to seal in the filling. Trim off excess pastry and use to make leaves to decorate the top of the pie. Pinch the edges of the pastry into a fluted edge. Brush the top of the pie with a little beaten egg.

Bake at 250 C using medium microwave setting for 10–12 minutes, or until the pastry is golden and the pie cooked through. Serve freshly cooked.

MEXICAN-STYLE TURKEY FILLETS

 HIGH

Combination:

 MEDIUM

 250 C

SERVES 4

Illustrated on page 23

1 green chilli, deseeded and chopped
1 large onion, chopped
2 large cloves garlic, crushed
2 tablespoons oil
salt and freshly ground black pepper
4 (225-g/8-oz) turkey breast fillets

4 tomatoes, peeled and chopped
2 avocados, halved, stone removed, peeled and chopped
juice of ½ lemon
150 ml/¼ pint soured cream

Put the chilli, onion, garlic and oil in a basin and cover. Cook using microwaves only on high for 3 minutes. Stir in the seasoning. Heat the oven to 250 C.

Arrange the turkey fillets in a flan dish and top with the onion mixture. Cook at 250 C using medium microwave setting for 10 minutes. Meanwhile, mix the tomato, avocado and lemon juice. Season to taste. Turn the turkey fillets over and top with the tomato mixture. Cook for a further 10 minutes, or until the turkey is cooked through. Spoon the soured cream over and serve at once, with a mixture of boiled rice and red kidney beans.

BONED STUFFED TURKEY

 HIGH

Combination:

 MEDIUM

 200 C

SERVES 8

◆ If you have a good butcher, then ask him to bone out the turkey for you. If you are attempting the task yourself just set aside enough time and take it slowly!

If cranberries are not available use bottled cranberry sauce in the stuffing, pepping it up with a dash of brandy if you like.

1 (4.5-kg/10-lb) turkey
175 g/6 oz cranberries
40 g/1½ oz sugar
2 tablespoons orange juice
225 g/8 oz onions, finely chopped
50 g/2 oz butter

225 g/8 oz fresh breadcrumbs
1 tablespoon rubbed sage
150 ml/¼ pint milk
salt and freshly ground black pepper
450 g/1 lb pork sausagemeat

Trim the leg and wing ends off the turkey. To bone the turkey, place it breast side down on a large clean work surface. Using a sharp, pointed knife, cut straight down the middle of the back, from head to tail. Working on one side, cut off all the meat, as near to the bone as possible. Take time and use the point of the knife to cut the meat away from the bones. Take great care not to puncture the skin. When you come to the leg and wing, carefully scrape the meat down the joints. As you near the ends of the joints, turn the meat and skin inside out to leave the bones completely cleaned. Carefully work round underneath the breast meat, cleaning the ribs as far as the main breast bone. Now leave the first side and remove the meat from the second side in the same way.

When you reach the breast bone, very carefully cut the finest sliver of bone off to separate the carcass completely from the meat without cutting the skin at all. The bones can be used along with the giblets to make an excellent stock.

Prepare the stuffings: put the cranberries in a basin with the sugar and orange juice. Cover and cook using microwaves only on high for 3 minutes. Stir well. Put the onion in a bowl with the butter and cook on high for 5 minutes. Stir the breadcrumbs, sage and milk into the onion, adding plenty of seasoning.

Lay the boned turkey, skin side down, flat on the surface. Spread the sausagemeat thinly and evenly over it. Spread the sage and onion stuffing evenly over the sausagemeat to cover the turkey completely. Spread the cranberry sauce down the middle, then carefully lift the sides of the turkey over the cranberry mixture to enclose it completely within the other stuffings.

Using a trussing needle or large darning needle and buttonhole thread, sew up the bird, then turn it over so that the breast meat is uppermost. Press it into a neat shape, tucking the wing and leg ends underneath and plumping up the middle. Place in a large flan dish.

Roast at 200 C using medium microwave setting for 30 minutes. Turn the turkey over, drain off any excess fat and cook for a further 30 minutes. Turn the turkey again so that the breast side is uppermost and cook for a final 15–20 minutes, or until the meat is cooked through. Test whether the turkey is cooked by piercing it at the thickest part – there should be no sign of any pink meat and the juices should run clear.

Leave to stand for 15 minutes, then serve hot. Alternatively, the turkey can be served cold.

Top Braised Pheasant (page 34)
Bottom Boned Stuffed Turkey (this page)

TURKEY DRUMSTICKS WITH SPROUTS AND BACON

 HIGH

Combination:

 MEDIUM

 250 C

SERVES 4

1 onion, finely chopped
225 g/8 oz rindless bacon, chopped
25 g/1 oz butter
1 clove garlic, crushed
½ teaspoon rubbed sage

½ teaspoon dried thyme
salt and freshly ground black pepper
4 (225-g/8-oz) drumsticks
675 g/1½ lb sprouts, trimmed and halved
150 ml/¼ pint dry cider

Put the onion and bacon in a casserole dish. Cover and cook using microwaves only on high for 5 minutes. Meanwhile, cream the butter with the garlic, herbs and seasoning. Spread this mixture all over the turkey drumsticks. Heat the oven to 250 C.

Add the sprouts and cider to the bacon and onion, stir well and arrange the drumsticks on top. Cook at 250 C using medium microwave setting for 10 minutes. Turn the drumsticks over and rearrange the sprout mixture as far as possible. Cook for a further 10–15 minutes. Serve freshly cooked with a potato dish, rice or pasta.

DUCK CREOLE

 HIGH

Combination:

 MEDIUM

 250 C

SERVES 4

◆ If you are unsure about your talents for jointing a cooked duck then buy duck joints. Cook the rice first, then reheat it using microwaves only on high just before serving.

½ teaspoon chilli powder
½ teaspoon ground ginger
1 teaspoon ground coriander
½ teaspoon salt
2 cloves garlic, crushed
1 (1.75–2-kg/4–4½-lb) duck
1 small onion, halved

Sauce
1 green pepper, deseeded and chopped
2 tablespoons plain flour
1 (432-g/15¼-oz) can pineapple chunks in
    natural juice
150 ml/¼ pint boiling water
salt and freshly ground black pepper

Mix the spices, salt and garlic. Place the duck on a flan dish. Cut away any excess fat and put the onion halves in the body cavity. Prick the skin all over, then rub the spice mixture well into the duck. Roast breast-uppermost at 250 C using medium microwave setting for 10 minutes. Turn the duck over and cook for a further 10 minutes. Turn the duck again so that the breast is uppermost. Drain off the excess fat and cook for a further 10 minutes, or until the duck is cooked and browned.

Remove the duck from the dish and keep hot. Drain off the excess fat, then stir the green pepper with the cooking juices. Cook using microwaves only on high for 3 minutes. Stir in the flour, pineapple and juice and the water. Add seasoning to taste. Cook using microwaves only on high for 3–5 minutes, or until the sauce is boiling.

While the sauce is cooking, use a pair of kitchen scissors and a sharp knife to joint the duck. Serve the duck on cooked rice with the sauce poured over.

DUCK WITH ORANGE AND TARRAGON SAUCE

Combination:

 MEDIUM

◆ 250 C

SERVES 4

Illustrated on page 23

◆ This is a slight variation on a very traditional recipe. The addition of a little tarragon lifts the sauce into the realms of the unusual. Serve with rice or pasta instead of a potato dish.

1 (1.75–2-kg/4–4½-lb) oven-ready duck
1 large orange, quartered
1 small onion, quartered
4 cloves
salt and freshly ground black pepper
Sauce
2 tablespoons plain flour
coarsely grated rind and juice of 1 orange

300 ml/½ pint stock (made from the duck giblets, or chicken stock)
150 ml/¼ pint dry sherry
1 tablespoon dried or 2 tablespoons chopped fresh tarragon
Garnish
1 orange, cut into wedges
sprigs of fresh tarragon or watercress

Trim any excess fat from the duck. Put the orange and onion quarters in the body cavity with the cloves. Prick the skin all over, then rub salt over the bird. Place breast uppermost in a flan dish or any flat dish that fits into the oven.

Cook at 250 C using medium microwave setting for 10 minutes. Turn the duck over and drain off any excess fat if necessary. Cook for a further 10 minutes. Again, drain off any fat which is likely to overflow from the dish, turn the duck over so that the breast is uppermost. Cook for a final 10–12 minutes. The skin should be crisp and browned. Pierce the duck at the thickest point. The juices should be free of blood when the bird is cooked. Transfer the duck to a heated serving dish. Cover with foil, placing the shiny side inwards to reflect the heat back towards the bird. Do not wrap the bird tightly or the skin will loose its crisp texture.

Drain the fat from the cooking dish, reserving the juices. Stir in the flour, then add the orange rind and juice and whisk well. Gradually whisk in the stock and sherry. If you find the dish awkward to lift when full of liquid, then pour the sauce ingredients into a basin, making sure that all the goodness is scraped off the dish. Add the tarragon and cook using microwaves only on high for 3–5 minutes, or until the sauce is boiling. Taste and adjust the seasoning.

Garnish the duck with wedges of orange and tarragon or watercress sprigs. Serve the sauce separately.

VARIATION
Duck with Grapefruit and Ginger Omit the orange from the body cavity, using just the onion and cloves. For the sauce, use the grated rind and juice of 1 grapefruit instead of the orange. Omit the tarragon but finely chop and add 2 pieces of preserved stem ginger and 2 tablespoons of the syrup instead.

CRANBERRY PHEASANT

 HIGH

Combination:

 MEDIUM

 200 C

SERVES 4

◆ This is a good recipe for when cranberries are in season. For use throughout the year keep a packet of the berries in the freezer; cook from frozen for an extra minute or so.

100 g/4 oz cranberries
1 onion, chopped
4 tablespoons sugar
2 tablespoons port
2 firm pears, peeled, cored and chopped
50 g/2 oz fresh breadcrumbs
salt and freshly ground black pepper

2 oven-ready pheasant
2 bay leaves
4 rashers rindless bacon
Sauce
2 tablespoons plain flour
300 ml/½ pint red wine
150 ml/¼ pint boiling water

Put the cranberries and onion in a basin. Cover with microwave cling film or a plate and cook using microwaves only on high for 5 minutes. Heat the oven to 200 C.

Mix the sugar, port, pears and breadcrumbs into the cranberry and onion mixture. Add seasoning to taste. Thoroughly rinse and dry the pheasant. Spoon the stuffing into the birds, then place in a flan dish. Top with bay leaves and bacon.

Roast at 200 C using medium microwave setting for 20 minutes. Remove the bacon from the top of the birds, putting it beside them in the dish. Remove and reserve the bay leaves. Roast the pheasant for a further 5 minutes, or until cooked.

Transfer the pheasant to a warmed serving dish and keep hot. Crumble the bacon into the cooking juices and stir in the flour. Stir in the wine and boiling water, then cook using microwaves only on high for 5 minutes, or until the sauce has boiled and thickened slightly. Taste and adjust the seasoning before serving.

BRAISED PHEASANT

Combination:

 MEDIUM

 200 C

SERVES 4

Illustrated on page 23

2 oven-ready pheasant
1 orange, quartered
12 cloves
1 onion, finely chopped
2 bay leaves
300 ml/½ pint red wine
2 rashers rindless bacon, halved

25 g/1 oz butter
2 tablespoons plain flour
salt and freshly ground black pepper
Garnish
1 orange, sliced
parsley sprigs

Heat the oven to 200 C. Rinse and dry the pheasant. Stud the orange quarters with the cloves, then place two pieces in each pheasant. Put the onion in a large casserole dish with the bay leaves. Place the pheasant on top, with the breasts uppermost. Pour the wine over and lay the bacon pieces on top of the pheasant.

Cook at 200 C using medium microwave setting for 20 minutes. Turn the pheasant over and cook for a further 10 minutes. Turn the birds once more and cook for a final 5–10 minutes, with the bacon removed. Meanwhile, beat the butter and flour together with seasoning to taste. Transfer the cooked pheasant to a serving platter and keep hot. Whisk the butter and flour mixture into the cooking juices. Cook using microwaves only on high for 3–5 minutes, or until boiling. Garnish the pheasant with orange slices and parsley sprigs. Serve the sauce separately.

Spinach-stuffed Lamb (page 41)

· MEAT ·
DISHES

MEAT ROASTING CHART

MEAT	MICROWAVE POWER SETTING	TEMPERATURE °C	TIME IN MINUTES PER 450 G/1 LB	INSTRUCTIONS NOTE: No need to preheat oven for cooking times over 30 minutes.
BEEF Rump Steak – medium/well done	Medium	240–250	5–6	Preheat oven. Brush steak with a little oil and place on rack or in a large shallow dish. Turn over halfway through cooking.
Rump Steak – well-done	Medium	240–250	7–8	As above
Topside/Sirloin	Medium	180	12–15	Place joint in dish or on rack. Turn and baste twice during cooking.
Rolled Rib	Medium	180	12–15	As above
Rib on the Bone	Medium	180	10–12	Turn joint and baste once or twice during cooking.
Brisket	Medium	220–180	14–15	Place meat on bed of diced vegetables (onion, carrot and potato). Add 150–300 ml/$\frac{1}{4}$–$\frac{1}{2}$ pint water and season. Cook at 220 for 15 minutes, then reduce temperature for remaining time. Turn twice during cooking.
LAMB Chops	Medium	240–250	7–9	Preheat oven. Arrange chops in dish, sprinkle with herbs. Turn over halfway through cooking.
Steaks (Slices off the leg)	Medium	240–250	10–12	As above
Leg	Medium	190	9–11	Season the joint and place in a dish. Turn and baste two or three times during cooking.
Shoulder	Medium	200	10–12	As above
Breast, boned and rolled	Medium	220	13–14	As above
PORK Chops	Medium	240–250	7–9	Preheat oven. Arrange in dish and season. Turn halfway through cooking.
Loin, boned and rolled	Medium	220–190	14–16	Score rind, rub with salt and place pork in dish. Reduce temperature after 15 minutes. Baste frequently, turn twice, having rind uppermost for 5 minutes at the end of cooking time. Increase temperature again for last 5 minutes. Leave to stand for 5–10 minutes before serving.
Loin, on the bone	Medium	220–190	15–16	Score rind and rub with salt. Place pork in dish, rind uppermost. Cook as above, reducing temperature after 5 minutes. Increase temperature at the end of cooking if the rind needs crisping.
Leg	Medium	220–180	15–16	Rub rind with salt and score well. Place in dish. Reduce temperature after 5 minutes. Baste frequently, turn twice during cooking.
Pork Belly	Medium	240–250	10	Score rind, rub with salt. Place in dish and turn twice during cooking. Have rind uppermost to start, underneath for the majority of cooking, then on top for final 3–5 minutes.
GAMMON	Medium	200–180	15–18	Place in deep casserole or mixing bowl. Add chopped onion, carrot and bay leaf. Pour in 300–600 ml/$\frac{1}{2}$–1 pint boiling water. Cover. Turn joint twice during cooking. Reduce temperature halfway through cooking. Leave to stand for 15 minutes.

ROAST BEEF WITH YORKSHIRE PUDDING AND ROAST POTATOES

To cook a traditional meal of this type, par-cook the potatoes first in an ovenproof dish using microwaves only on high. Add a little fat. Put the meat on the rack above the potatoes (in a dish if you like) and cook for the necessary time. Make up a quantity of batter as for Toads-in-Holes (see page 60). Remove the meat and heat a little of the dripping in a quiche dish. Pour in the batter and cook for 10–15 minutes at 250 C using medium microwave setting. The potatoes and Yorkshire pudding will be ready together; make the gravy using microwaves only just before serving.

BEEF WELLINGTON

 HIGH

Combination:

 MEDIUM

 250 C

SERVES 4–6

◆ This is an expensive dish to prepare but it is truly delicious. If you like, use a neat piece of topside instead of the fillet steak. Other suitable substitutions are a piece of lean boneless lamb, cut from the leg, or a piece of pork, trimmed of all fat. If using pork, then remember to cook it well first.

1 kg/2 lb fillet steak
1 large onion, finely chopped
1 clove garlic, crushed (optional)
knob of butter
100 g/4 oz button mushrooms, chopped

1 tablespoon chopped parsley
salt and freshly ground black pepper
1 (370-g/13-oz) packet puff pastry, defrosted
   if frozen
1 egg, beaten

Tie the piece of steak firmly in shape so that it does not curve as it cooks. Place the onion and garlic (if used) in a basin with the butter. Cook using microwaves only on high for 3 minutes. Heat the oven to 250 C.

Mix the mushroom and parsley into the onion, adding a generous sprinkling of seasoning. Place the meat on a flan dish and cook at 250 C using medium microwave setting for 5–10 minutes. The length of time for this initial cooking period depends on how well done you like your beef. If you like it just red in the middle and quite juicy, then 5 minutes is long enough; for a result which is slightly pink in the middle, allow 7–8 minutes and for well-done steak cook for the full 10 minutes. Remove the meat from the oven and set aside to cool.

Roll out the pastry on a lightly floured surface into an oblong large enough to enclose the meat completely. It should measure about 30 × 40 cm/12 × 16 in and be fairly thick. Spread the mushroom mixture in the middle of the pastry. Remove the string from the meat and place the steak on top of the mushroom mixture. Lift the pastry over the meat to ensure that it fits, then trim off square shapes from each corner to avoid having any very thick pastry joins.

Brush the edges of the pastry with a little of the beaten egg, then fold the pastry around the meat, pressing the joins firmly together. Turn the package over and place it on a large flan dish. From the pastry trimmings cut a few leaves to place on top of the Beef Wellington. Glaze the pastry with beaten egg and bake at 250 C using medium microwave setting for about 12 minutes, or until the pastry is well puffed and browned. Serve freshly cooked, cut into slices.

MINCED BEEF PIE

 HIGH

Combination:

 MEDIUM

 220 C

SERVES 4

1 large onion, chopped
100 g/4 oz carrots, diced
1 tablespoon oil
salt and freshly ground black pepper
100 g/4 oz mushrooms, sliced
450 g/1 lb minced beef
1 tablespoon tomato purée

½ teaspoon dried or 1 teaspoon chopped
  fresh thyme
2 tablespoons chopped parsley
bay leaf
250 ml/8 fl oz boiling water
1 quantity Shortcrust Pastry (page 68)
beaten egg to glaze

Place the onion, carrot and oil in a pie dish and cover with a plate or with microwave cling film. Cook using microwaves only on high for 5 minutes. Heat the oven to 220 C. Add a good sprinkling of seasoning to the onion and carrot, then mix in the mushroom and beef. Stir the tomato purée and herbs into the boiling water, then pour the liquid over the meat mixture. Set aside.

Roll out the pastry on a lightly floured surface into a piece large enough to cover the top of the pie dish with about 2.5 cm/1 in all round to spare. Trim a narrow strip from the edge of the pastry, then dampen the edge of the dish and press the strip of pastry on to it. Lift the pastry lid over the filling, pressing the edges down well. Trim off excess pastry and re-roll it to make decorative leaves to put on top of the pie.

Brush the pie with a little beaten egg and bake at 220 C using medium microwave setting for about 15–18 minutes or until well browned. Serve piping hot, with baked potatoes and a crunchy green vegetable to make a satisfying winter's meal.

BEEF LASAGNE

 HIGH

Combination:

 MEDIUM

 200 C

SERVES 4

◆ Minced pork or lamb, or finely chopped cooked chicken are good substitutes for beef in this lasagne.

1 large onion, chopped
2 cloves garlic, crushed
1 tablespoon oil
salt and freshly ground black pepper
450 g/1 lb minced beef
1 (397-g/14-oz) can chopped tomatoes

1 teaspoon dried marjoram
100 g/4 oz button mushrooms, chopped
175 g/6 oz no precook lasagne
450 ml/¾ pint Cheese Sauce (page 120)
50 g/2 oz cheese, grated
2 tablespoons dry breadcrumbs

Put the onion in a large basin or casserole dish with the garlic and oil. Cook using microwaves only on high for 3 minutes. Stir in plenty of seasoning, the beef, tomatoes, marjoram and mushroom. Continue to cook on high for 5 minutes, then stir well. Heat the oven to 200 C.

For the lasagne you will need a deep casserole dish that will fit into the oven. If you have a large oven cavity that does not have a turntable then you can use an ordinary, large lasagne dish. I found that cooking the lasagne in a deep round dish gave an excellent result – very moist, without bubbling over at the edges.

Layer the pieces of lasagne, breaking them up as necessary, with the meat sauce in the dish. Pour the cheese sauce on top. Mix the cheese with the breadcrumbs and sprinkle over the top of the lasagne. Bake at 200 C using medium microwave setting for 25–30 minutes or until well browned on top and cooked through. To check that the lasagne is cooked, pierce the middle with the point of a knife – the pasta should feel softened. Serve freshly baked, with a crisp fresh salad.

GINGERED LAMB WITH MANGO

 HIGH

Combination:

 MEDIUM

 190 C

SERVES 6

1 (1.75-kg/3¾-lb) leg of lamb
50 g/2 oz fresh root ginger, sliced
salt and freshly ground black pepper
grated rind and juice of 1 orange

1 tablespoon plain flour
300 ml/½ pint dry white wine or dry cider
1 mango, just ripe but not too soft

Make small cuts under the skin on the lamb – do not cut deeply into the meat but make the cuts at an angle to create pockets under the skin. Press the ginger slices into the pockets – for this recipe there is no need to peel the ginger because it is not going to be eaten. Sprinkle the meat with seasoning and place it in a flan dish that will fit into the oven. Sprinkle the orange juice over.

Roast the lamb at 190 C using medium microwave setting for 30–40 minutes. Turn the joint once or twice during cooking so that it browns evenly. Baste the top on each occasion. Pierce the meat to make sure that it is cooked to your liking, allowing for the fact that 5 minutes standing time at the end of cooking will make a slight difference and may well complete the cooking to the well-done stage.

Wrap the meat in foil, shiny side inwards, and make the sauce. Drain off any excess fat from the cooking dish and stir in the flour. Add the grated orange rind. Gradually pour in the wine or cider, stirring all the time. Cook using microwaves only for 4 minutes, or until boiling and thickened.

While the sauce cooks, peel the mango and cut the flesh off the stone in slices. Add the fruit to the sauce and taste for seasoning. Heat for 1 minute before serving. As you carve the lamb remove the pieces of ginger, then spoon a little sauce over each portion.

STUFFED BREAST OF LAMB

 HIGH

Combination:

 MEDIUM

 220 C

SERVES 4

1 small onion, finely chopped
225 g/8 oz cooking apples, peeled, cored and chopped
2 teaspoons clear honey
75 g/3 oz fresh breadcrumbs
salt and freshly ground black pepper

¼ teaspoon ground cloves
25 g/1 oz raisins
2 teaspoons chopped rosemary
about 3 tablespoons dry cider
1 (675-g/1½-lb) breast of lamb, boned

Put the onion in a basin, cover and cook using microwaves only on high for 3 minutes. Heat the oven to 220 C.

For the stuffing, mix all the remaining ingredients, except the lamb, with the onion, adding enough cider to bind. Lay the lamb flat on a board and trim off any excess fat. Spread the stuffing over in a thick layer. Roll up carefully and tie with thread, taking care not to squeeze the stuffing out. Place in a flan dish and rub a little salt into the outside of the joint.

Roast at 220 C using medium microwave setting for 20–25 minutes, or until the lamb is cooked through and well browned on the outside. Use the cooking juices to make a gravy and serve the lamb sliced.

SPINACH-STUFFED LAMB

Combination:

 MEDIUM

 200 C

SERVES 6

Illustrated on page 35

◆ Spinach makes an excellent stuffing for lamb, particularly when flavoured with garlic. There is a rich wine sauce to accompany this roast but if preferred, make a simple gravy using stock or water.

225 g/8 oz frozen spinach, defrosted, or 1 kg/ 2 lb fresh spinach, cooked, thoroughly drained and chopped (see page 117 for cooking instructions)
75 g/3 oz fresh breadcrumbs
1 onion, chopped
2 cloves garlic, crushed
100 g/4 oz mushrooms, chopped
salt and freshly ground black pepper

1 (1.5-kg/3-lb) shoulder of lamb, boned
a few sprigs of fresh rosemary
Rich Wine Sauce
2 tablespoons plain flour
150 ml/¼ pint boiling water
300 ml/½ pint full-bodied red wine
1 tablespoon tomato purée
generous dash of Worcestershire sauce

Mix the spinach with the breadcrumbs, onion, garlic and mushroom. Add seasoning to taste. Use a spoon to press this mixture into the lamb. Use a trussing or darning needle and strong thread to sew up the lamb and seal in the stuffing.

Place the lamb on a large flan dish and sprinkle the rosemary on top. Roast at 200 C using medium microwave setting for 20 minutes. Turn the lamb over and continue to cook for 15 minutes. Turn the lamb again and cook for a final 10 minutes. Each time you turn the lamb, check to make sure that there is no danger of fat spilling over.

Wrap the cooked lamb in foil, shiny side inwards. Drain off excess fat and stir the flour into the cooking juices. Stir in the boiling water and wine, then whisk in the tomato purée and Worcestershire sauce. Cook using microwaves only on high for 5 minutes, whisk well and taste. Adjust the seasoning, then cook for a further 2–3 minutes, or until the sauce is boiling and slightly thickened. Transfer the lamb to a serving dish and garnish with fresh rosemary if you like. Serve the sauce separately. Remember to remove the thread as you carve the lamb.

CROWN ROAST

 HIGH

Combination:

 MEDIUM

 220 C

SERVES 6–8

1 onion, finely chopped
1 (425-g/15-oz) can peach slices, drained and chopped
bunch of watercress, trimmed and chopped
grated rind and juice of 1 orange
salt and freshly ground black pepper

100 g/4 oz fresh breadcrumbs
1 crown roast, prepared from 2 racks of lamb, each having 7 cutlets
Garnish
1 orange, cut into wedges
watercress sprigs

Put the onion in a basin, cover and cook using microwaves only on high for 3 minutes. Mix in the remaining ingredients apart from the lamb. Heat the oven to 220 C. The butcher will prepare the crown roast for you, but make sure that the inside does not contain too thick a layer of fat. Stand the meat on a flan dish. Press the stuffing into the crown roast and roast at 220 C using medium microwave setting for 25–30 minutes. To check that the meat is cooked, carefully pierce one of the cutlets at the base with the point of a knife.

Transfer the roast to a warmed serving platter. Make gravy from the meat juices or use them as the basis for a red wine sauce (see page 120). Arrange the garnish around the base of the crown roast and stick a cutlet frill on each of the bones. To serve, use a sharp knife to cut between the cutlets.

LANCASHIRE HOT POT

  HIGH

Combination:

 MEDIUM

◆ 220 C

SERVES 4

1 kg/2 lb best end neck of lamb, chopped into pieces
2 tablespoons plain flour
salt and freshly ground black pepper
bay leaf
sprig of thyme

parsley sprig
1 onion, finely chopped
600 ml/1 pint boiling water
675 g/1½ lb potatoes, sliced
knob of butter or margarine

Trim any excess fat off the meat. Put the pieces in a polythene bag, then sprinkle in the flour and plenty of seasoning. Shake the bag well to coat the meat in the seasoned flour. Put the meat in a large casserole dish, adding any leftover flour. Add the herbs and onion, then pour in the boiling water. Top with the potato, overlapping the slices.

Dot with butter or margarine and cook using microwaves only on high for 10 minutes. Continue cooking at 220 C using medium microwave setting for 25–30 minutes, or until the meat is tender and the potato crisp and brown. Serve with buttered cabbage, cauliflower or peas.

ALTERNATIVE METHOD
Cook using microwaves only on high for 10 minutes as above, then cook at 200 C and low microwave setting for about 40 minutes.

SPICY LAMB STRIPS

Combination:

 MEDIUM

 250 C

SERVES 4

◆ These are great as a starter or, served with Basmati rice and cucumber with yogurt, for a light meal.

1 (675-g/1½-lb) breast of lamb, chopped into strips
1 small onion, finely chopped
1 tablespoon ground coriander
1 teaspoon ground cumin
½ teaspoon ground ginger
generous pinch of chilli powder (or more if you have a taste for heat)

salt and freshly ground black pepper
Garnish
fresh coriander leaves
1 lemon, cut into wedges

Heat the oven to 250 C. Trim excess fat from the lamb. Mix all the remaining ingredients and spread the mixture over the lamb. Place in a flan dish. If you have the time, leave the meat to marinate for a few hours to enhance the flavour. Bake at 250 C using medium microwave setting for 10 minutes. Turn the pieces of lamb and cook for a further 5–7 minutes or until browned and sizzling.

Serve freshly cooked, garnished with coriander leaves and lemon wedges. The juice from the lemon adds zest to the rich, spicy lamb.

LAMB CHOPS WITH WALNUTS AND MARJORAM

Combination:

 MEDIUM

◆ 250 C

SERVES 4

50 g/2 oz walnuts, chopped
1 tablespoon chopped fresh marjoram
50 g/2 oz fresh breadcrumbs
salt and freshly ground black pepper

4 lamb chump chops
Garnish
1 tomato, sliced
fresh herb sprigs (ideally marjoram)

Heat the oven to 250 C. Mix all the ingredients apart from the chops. Arrange the chops on a flan dish and roast at 250 C using medium microwave setting for 5 minutes.

Turn the chops over and press a quarter of the walnut herb mixture on top of each one. Cook at 250 C using medium microwave setting for a further 10 minutes, or until the lamb is cooked. Serve at once, garnished with slices of tomato and sprigs of fresh herbs.

STUFFED LEG OF LAMB

 HIGH

Combination:

 MEDIUM

◆ 190 C

SERVES 6

1 (1.75-kg/3¾-lb) leg of lamb, boned
225 g/8 oz ready-to-eat dried prunes, roughly chopped
4 tablespoons brandy
1 large onion, chopped
25 g/1 oz butter
100 g/4 oz fresh breadcrumbs
salt and freshly ground black pepper

100 g/4 oz button mushrooms, chopped
1 teaspoon dried mixed herbs
Sauce
2 tablespoons plain flour
300 ml/½ pint red wine
300 ml/½ pint boiling water
bay leaf

Place the lamb in a large flan dish. Put the prunes in a basin and sprinkle the brandy over them. Set aside. Put the onion and butter in a basin and cook using microwaves only on high for 3 minutes. Stir in the breadcrumbs, seasoning and mushroom. Add the herbs, then the prunes and brandy. Mix well, then press this stuffing into the lamb.

Roast the lamb at 190 C using medium microwave setting for 35–45 minutes. Turn the joint twice during cooking, basting it with the cooking juices. Pierce the joint with a pointed knife at the thickest part to make sure that it is cooked to your liking. Transfer to a serving platter and keep hot.

Drain off the excess fat, then stir the flour into the cooking juices. Gradually pour in the wine and water and add the bay leaf. If the dish is too shallow to contain the sauce, then pour it into a large basin, making sure that all the cooking juices are scraped off the dish. Cook using microwaves only on high for 8 minutes, whisking well once during cooking. Taste and adjust the seasoning, then serve the sauce with the lamb.

ROAST PORK WITH APPLE AND ONION SAUCE

Combination:

 MEDIUM

 250 C

SERVES 4

1-kg/2–2¼-lb piece belly of pork
4 cloves garlic
2 onions, chopped
2 large cooking apples, peeled, cored and
  thickly sliced

1 tablespoon chopped rosemary
salt and freshly ground black pepper
1 tablespoon sugar

Heat the oven to 250 C. Make sure the rind of the pork is well scored. Make a few slits on the underside, not into the rind, of the pork. Tuck the cloves of garlic into the meat. Put the onions and apples in a flan dish and place the pork on top, rind uppermost. Sprinkle with the rosemary and seasoning. Roast at 250 C using medium microwave setting for 10 minutes. Turn the joint over and cook for a further 10 minutes then turn it back again and cook for a final 10 minutes. Do not disturb the apples as you turn the pork.

Transfer the pork to a warmed serving plate. Drain all the fat off the apples and onions (reserving the cooking juices to make gravy) and transfer them to a basin. Beat the apples and onions with the sugar and add a little seasoning. Serve this apple sauce with the pork.

BARBECUE SPARERIBS

Combination:

 MEDIUM

 250 C

SERVES 4

2 tablespoons tomato purée
4 tablespoons soy sauce
2 tablespoons soft brown sugar
2 cloves garlic, crushed

1 onion, grated
2 teaspoons prepared mustard
1 kg/2 lb pork spareribs, separated

Heat the oven to 250 C. Mix all the ingredients apart from the spareribs. Place the ribs in a large flan dish and brush the sauce over. Roast at 250 C using medium microwave setting for 10 minutes. Turn the ribs over and baste with sauce, then cook for a further 10–15 minutes, or until well browned and tender. Serve piping hot.

PORK LOIN BOULANGÈRE

SERVES 6

◆ When making the sauce, you will probably find that there is too much liquid for a flan dish, so pour into a large basin. A recipe for Sprouts with chestnuts, in our photograph, is on page 116.

1.75 kg/4 lb loin of pork (on the bone)
½ teaspoon ground cloves
salt and freshly ground black pepper
800 g/1¾ lb potatoes, thickly sliced
2 onions, thinly sliced
2 teaspoons rubbed sage

Cider Sauce
2 tablespoons plain flour
450 ml/¾ pint dry cider
50 g/2 oz button mushrooms, sliced
150 ml/¼ pint single cream

Make sure that the rind of the pork is well scored. Rub the ground cloves and plenty of seasoning into the rind. Layer the potato and onion slices in a large flan dish and sprinkle with the sage. Place the joint of pork on top. Roast at 220 C using medium microwave setting for 30 minutes. Turn the joint over so that the rind is underneath and reduce the temperature to 190 C. Continue cooking using medium microwave setting for 30 minutes. Rearrange the potato and onion and turn the joint rind side uppermost. Increase the temperature to 220 C and use medium microwave setting for a final 5–7 minutes, or until the meat is cooked and the rind crisp.

Transfer the meat to a serving platter and use a slotted spoon to arrange the potatoes and onion around it. Cover with foil, shiny side inwards. Drain off the fat and stir the flour into the cooking juices. Whisk in the cider, scraping the sides of the dish. Add the mushroom and cook using microwaves only on high for 7–10 minutes, or until boiling and slightly thickened. Stir in the cream and taste for seasoning. Heat for 2 minutes without allowing the sauce to boil.

STUFFED PORK CHOPS

HIGH

Combination:

MEDIUM

250 C

SERVES 4

1 onion, finely chopped
50 g/2 oz no-need-to-soak dried apricots
50 g/2 oz blanched almonds, chopped
50 g/2 oz fresh breadcrumbs
salt and freshly ground black pepper

2 teaspoons chopped rosemary
100 ml/4 fl oz milk
4 (225-g/8-oz) thick pork chops
watercress sprigs to garnish

Put the onion in a basin and cook using microwaves only on high for 3 minutes. Stir in all the remaining ingredients apart from the chops. Heat the oven to 250 C.

Trim excess fat from the chops, then make a horizontal slit into each one as far as the bone but without slitting the ends. You should have a good-sized pocket in each chop. Divide the stuffing between the chops, using a teaspoon to press it into the pockets.

Arrange the chops in a flan dish and roast at 250 C using medium microwave setting for 7 minutes. Turn the chops over and cook for a further 7 minutes. Serve garnished with watercress sprigs. Fantail potatoes (see page 53) make a good accompaniment.

Use the cooking juices to make a gravy, as described in the recipe on page 120.

PEPPERED PORK BRAISE

 HIGH

Combination:

 MEDIUM

◆ 250 C

SERVES 4

1 large onion, halved and sliced
1 red pepper, deseeded and chopped
1 green pepper, deseeded and chopped
knob of butter
2 tablespoons plain flour

250 ml/8 fl oz red wine, dry cider or
   unsweetened apple juice
bay leaf
salt and freshly ground black pepper
4 pork chops, trimmed of excess fat

Put the onion and peppers in a casserole dish with the butter and cook using microwaves only on high for 5 minutes. Heat the oven to 250 C.

Stir the flour into the pepper mixture, then stir in the wine, cider or apple juice. Add the bay leaf and a little seasoning. Add the chops to the dish, arranging them so that they are half in the sauce and half out. Cook at 250 C using medium microwave setting for 10 minutes. Turn the chops and braise for a further 7–10 minutes, or until the chops are cooked. Serve hot, with buttered pasta or rice.

PORK CASSEROLE WITH DUMPLINGS

 HIGH

Combination:

 MEDIUM

 220 C

SERVES 4

1 large onion, chopped
1 green pepper, deseeded and chopped
1 tablespoon oil
175 g/6 oz carrots, sliced
2 tablespoons plain flour
450 g/1 lb lean boneless pork, cubed
bay leaf
salt and freshly ground black pepper

300 ml/$\frac{1}{2}$ pint boiling water
Dumplings
225 g/8 oz self-raising flour
100 g/4 oz shredded suet
1 tablespoon chopped chives
1 tablespoon chopped parsley
1 teaspoon mustard powder
150 ml/$\frac{1}{4}$ pint water

Put the onion, green pepper and oil in a large casserole dish. Mix in the carrot, cover and cook using microwaves only on high for 5 minutes.

Add the flour to the vegetables and stir well. Mix in the pork, add the bay leaf and plenty of seasoning, then pour in the water, stirring all the time. Continue cooking using microwaves only on high for 5 minutes. Heat the oven to 220 C.

Meanwhile, make the dumplings: put the flour in a bowl with the suet. Mix in the herbs and mustard, then add the water and stir to make a sticky dough.

Cook the pork, without the dumplings, at 220 C using medium microwave setting for 5 minutes. Stir well, moving the pieces of meat from the edge of the dish into the middle. Shape the suet pastry into eight round dumplings and place them on top of the casserole. Continue cooking for a further 8–10 minutes, or until the pork is cooked and the dumplings are risen and lightly browned. Serve freshly cooked.

PORK AND PEANUT LOAF

 HIGH

Combination:

 MEDIUM

 200 C

SERVES 4

◆ This is delicious — vaguely reminiscent of satay recipes. The cooking time and temperature will be more or less the same for any meat loaf of this size. Try, for example, a combination of pork and spinach, beef with chopped fresh herbs or lamb with rosemary and grated potatoes.

1 large onion, finely chopped
2 large cloves garlic, crushed
1 tablespoon oil
salt and freshly ground black pepper
450 g/1 lb minced pork
100 g/4 oz salted peanuts, ground or very finely chopped
2 tablespoons soy sauce
50 g/2 oz fresh breadcrumbs

1 egg
½ teaspoon chilli powder (optional)
To serve
225 g/8 oz tomatoes, peeled and chopped
1 bunch spring onions, trimmed and chopped
1 teaspoon sugar
1 teaspoon red or white wine vinegar
salt and freshly ground black pepper

Place the onion and garlic in a basin with the oil. Cook using microwaves only on high for 3 minutes. Heat the oven to 200 C. Add a little seasoning, then mix in the pork, peanuts, soy sauce and breadcrumbs. When thoroughly combined add the egg and chilli powder, if using, and mix well.

Grease a 450-g/1-lb loaf dish and press the mixture into it. Bake at 200 C using medium microwave setting for 15 minutes, or until the pork and peanut loaf is cooked through. Leave in the dish for 5 minutes, then turn out the loaf and serve sliced.

While the meat loaf is cooking, mix the tomato with the spring onion, sugar and vinegar, adding seasoning to taste. Arrange the sliced meat loaf on a plate and top with the tomato mixture. Serve at once.

ALTERNATIVE METHOD
To cook at 200 C using a low microwave setting allow 20–25 minutes.

HONEY-BAKED GAMMON

Combination:

 MEDIUM

 200–180 C

SERVES 6–8

1.5–1.75-kg/3½–4-lb gammon joint
4 cloves
blade of mace

bay leaf
about 150 ml/¼ pint dry cider or water
2 tablespoons honey

Put the gammon joint in a large casserole dish or mixing bowl. Add the spices and bay leaf, then pour in enough cider or water to come about one-third of the way up the joint. The quantity of liquid will depend on the shape of the casserole dish.

Cover and cook at 200 C using medium microwave setting for 20 minutes. Turn the joint over and re-cover, then cook for a further 20 minutes. Reduce the oven temperature to 180 C and continue to cook using medium microwave setting for 10–15 minutes. Pierce the gammon underneath to check that it is almost cooked.

Remove the joint, discarding the cooking liquid (or reserve it to flavour a soup or stew), and cut off the rind. Mark the fat into diamond shapes and put the joint back in the casserole. Brush the honey over the gammon and cook at 180 C using medium microwave setting for a final 10 minutes. Leave to stand for 15 minutes before serving.

VEAL PAUPIETTES

Combination:

 MEDIUM

◆ 250 C

SERVES 4

◆ If you prefer, then you can use escalopes of pork or beaten cut chicken or turkey breast fillets instead of veal.

4 (100-g/4-oz) veal escalopes
2 slices cooked ham, cut in half
50 g/2 oz fresh breadcrumbs
75 g/3 oz mozzarella cheese, finely diced
1 tablespoon milk
½ teaspoon rubbed sage

salt and freshly ground black pepper
150 ml/¼ pint dry white wine
50 g/2 oz butter
2 tablespoons plain flour
150 ml/¼ pint single cream
sprigs of fresh sage to garnish (optional)

Heat the oven to 250 C. Lay the veal escalopes between two pieces of greaseproof paper and beat them out thinly. Use a meat mallet or rolling pin to do this.

Top each piece of veal with a piece of ham. Mix the breadcrumbs with the cheese, milk, sage and seasoning. Divide this stuffing between the veal and ham portions, piling it neatly in the middle on top of the ham. Fold the veal and ham around the stuffing to make a neat parcel. Tie each parcel neatly in place with cotton and place in a casserole dish. Pour in the wine and dot the veal with half the butter. Then bake at 250 C using medium microwave setting for 10 minutes or until the meat is cooked. Transfer the paupiettes to a serving dish.

Beat the flour with the remaining butter until a smooth thick paste is formed. Whisk this into the hot cooking liquid. Cook using microwaves only on high for 3 minutes. Beat the thickened sauce and add the cream. Heat using microwaves only on high again for a further 2 minutes, or until the sauce is hot but not boiling.

Pour the sauce over the paupiettes and garnish with sprigs of sage if you like. Serve with rice, pasta or new potatoes and a crisp salad.

LIVER AND BACON CASSEROLE

 HIGH

Combination:

 MEDIUM

◆ 220 C

SERVES 4

1 large onion, sliced
knob of butter
450 g/1 lb lamb's liver, sliced
225 g/8 oz rindless bacon, roughly chopped
2 tablespoons chopped parsley
1 teaspoon dried or 2 teaspoons chopped
  fresh thyme

salt and freshly ground black pepper
2 tablespoons tomato purée
2 teaspoons prepared mustard
300 ml/½ pint boiling water
25 g/1 oz butter or margarine

Put the onion in a basin with the butter and cook using microwaves only on high for 3 minutes. Heat the oven to 220 C.

Layer the liver and bacon with the onion and herbs in a casserole dish. End with a layer of bacon on top and sprinkle with seasoning. Mix the tomato purée and mustard with the boiling water, then pour it over the liver. Dot with the butter or margarine and bake at 220 C using medium microwave setting for 15 minutes, or until the liver is cooked through and the bacon on top is browned and slightly crisp.

Serve freshly cooked with baked potatoes or creamy mashed potatoes and French beans or peas.

Top *Souffléd Vegetable Bake* (page 57)
Bottom *Stuffed Aubergines* (page 56)

VEGETABLE
DISHES

CRISP BAKED POTATOES

Combination:

 HIGH

◇ 250 C

allow 1 (275-g/10-oz) potato per person

a little oil
butter to serve

Scrub the potatoes and cut out any eyes or bad bits. Brush with a little oil and place straight on the rack (or on a flat dish on the rack). Cook at 250 C using high microwave setting for the following times:

1 potato _____ 7 minutes
2 potatoes _____ 10 minutes
3 potatoes _____ 18 minutes
4 potatoes _____ 25 minutes
5 potatoes _____ 28–30 minutes
6 potatoes _____ 35 minutes

Serve the potatoes freshly cooked, split and topped with butter.

TATWS RHOST

Combination:

 MEDIUM

◇ 220 C

SERVES 4

675 g/1½ lb potatoes, thinly sliced
1 large onion, thinly sliced
225 g/8 oz rindless smoked bacon, roughly chopped

salt and freshly ground black pepper
2 tablespoons water
knob of butter

Layer the potato, onion and bacon in a dish, sprinkling the layers with a little salt and pepper. Sprinkle the water over the top, then dot with butter.

Bake at 220 C using medium microwave setting for 25–30 minutes, or until the potato is cooked through and the top is crisp and brown. Serve piping hot.

POTATOES LYONNAISE

Combination:

 MEDIUM

◇ 220 C

SERVES 4

350 g/12 oz onions, thinly sliced and separated into rings
450 g/1 lb potatoes, thinly sliced
salt and freshly ground black pepper

50 g/2 oz butter
5–6 tablespoons milk
2 tablespoons chopped parsley

Layer the onion rings and potato slices in a dish, seasoning each layer lightly. Dot with the butter and pour in the milk, then bake at 220 C using medium microwave setting for about 25 minutes, or until the potatoes are cooked through and browned on top. Sprinkle with chopped parsley and serve freshly cooked.

FANTAIL POTATOES

 HIGH

Combination:

 MEDIUM

 220 C

SERVES 4

8 medium potatoes
50 g/2 oz butter
salt and freshly ground black pepper

Peel and wash the potatoes, then cut them almost through into slices leaving all the slices attached at the base. Place in a flan dish and dot with butter. Sprinkle with seasoning and cook using microwaves only on high for 5 minutes.

Baste and continue to cook at 220 C using medium microwave setting for about 15 minutes, or until tender and browned. Serve freshly cooked.

STUFFED MARROW RINGS

 HIGH

Combination:

 MEDIUM

 200 C

SERVES 4

1 onion, chopped
knob of butter
4 (2.5-cm/1-in) thick slices marrow
450 g/1 lb minced beef
generous dash of Worcestershire sauce

100 g/4 oz carrots, grated
2 tablespoons chopped parsley
salt and freshly ground black pepper
50 g/2 oz cheese, grated
50 g/2 oz fresh breadcrumbs

Put the onion and butter in a basin and cook using microwaves only on high for 3 minutes. Peel the marrow slices and place them in a dish. Cover with microwave cling film and cook using microwaves only on high for 5 minutes. Heat the oven to 200 C. Mix the beef, Worcestershire sauce, carrot, parsley and seasoning with the onion. Divide between the marrow rings and bake, uncovered, at 200 C using medium microwave setting for 10 minutes.

Top the stuffing with a mixture of the cheese and breadcrumbs and continue to cook at 200 C using medium microwave setting for a further 5 minutes.

STUFFED COURGETTES

Combination:

MEDIUM

250 C

SERVES 4

4 courgettes
75 g/3 oz fresh breadcrumbs
100 g/4 oz cooked ham, chopped
2 tablespoons snipped chives
75 g/3 oz mozzarella cheese, finely diced

½ teaspoon oregano
salt and freshly ground black pepper
2 tablespoons milk
4 tomatoes, peeled and chopped, to garnish

Heat the oven to 250 C. Cut the courgettes in half and scoop out the middle. Chop the scooped out courgette and mix with the remaining ingredients. Put the courgette shells in two flat dishes and press the filling into the shells. Putting one dish straight on the turntable, the second on the wire rack, bake at 250 C using medium microwave power for 5 minutes. Swop the dishes over and cook for a further 5 minutes. Transfer to warmed plates and top with a little chopped tomato.

COURGETTE BAKE

Combination:

 MEDIUM

220 C

SERVES 4

◆ This bake can be served as a starter, as an accompaniment to grilled steak, veal chops or chicken, or as a mouth-watering supper dish. Offer plenty of warmed crusty bread with it if there is no other dish on the menu.

450 g/1 lb courgettes, sliced
225 g/8 oz tomatoes, peeled and sliced
50 g/2 oz cooked ham, roughly chopped
175 g/6 oz mozzarella cheese, thinly sliced
salt and freshly ground black pepper

1 teaspoon fennel seeds
1 teaspoon dried or 1 tablespoon chopped fresh basil
2 tablespoons olive oil

Heat the oven to 220 C. Layer the courgette and tomato slices with the ham, cheese, seasoning and fennel seeds in a dish. End with a layer of cheese, then sprinkle with basil and olive oil. Bake at 220 C using medium microwave setting for 10–12 minutes, or until browned on top and cooked. Serve at once.

VARIATION
Aubergines also taste rather good cooked in this bake. Take 2 aubergines, trim and slice them, then put the slices in a colander and sprinkle with salt. Leave for 30 minutes, rinse and shake dry. Place in a basin; cover and cook using microwaves only for 4–5 minutes. Layer up the aubergines as above, omitting the courgettes.

STUFFED PEPPERS

 HIGH

Combination:

 MEDIUM

◆ 200 C

SERVES 4

◆ These stuffed peppers are slightly spicy and are also good with soured cream and chives. If serving a tomato sauce remember to prepare and cook it in the microwave before cooking the peppers. Reheat the sauce briefly once the peppers are cooked.

1 onion, finely chopped
2 cloves garlic, crushed
1 tablespoon oil
450 g/1 lb minced beef
1 teaspoon ground coriander

$\frac{1}{2}$ teaspoon chilli powder
1 egg
175 g/6 oz cheese, grated
salt and freshly ground black pepper
4 large green or red peppers

Put the onion and garlic in a basin and add the oil. Cook using microwaves only on high for 3 minutes. Add the meat, spices, egg and three-quarters of the cheese. Mix thoroughly, adding seasoning to taste. Heat the oven to 200 C.

Cut a thin cap off the tops of the peppers. Discard all the pith and seeds from inside, rinse and dry. Fill the peppers with the meat mixture and place them in a casserole dish. Bake at 200 C using medium microwave setting for 10 minutes.

Sprinkle the remaining cheese on top of the peppers and continue to cook for a further 5 minutes. Serve hot, with a tomato sauce (see page 121).

VARIATION
Instead of the minced beef try using lean minced lamb, then serve the peppers with a sauce of grated cucumber mixed with that thick, Greek-style yogurt – Yum!!

STUFFED AUBERGINES

 HIGH

Combination:

 MEDIUM

 220 C

SERVES 4

Illustrated on page 51

2 large aubergines
salt and freshly ground black pepper
1 large onion, finely chopped
2 cloves garlic, crushed
2 tablespoons oil
450 g/1 lb minced pork
1 tablespoon tomato purée

$\frac{1}{2}$ teaspoon ground mace
$\frac{1}{2}$ teaspoon dried marjoram
50 ml/2 fl oz red wine
Topping
4 tablespoons soured cream
2 tablespoons roasted sesame seeds

Cut the aubergines in half. Cut criss-cross into the flesh, then use a teaspoon to scoop it out. Chop and place in a colander. Sprinkle with salt and leave to drain. Place the aubergine shells in a large flan dish.

Put the onion and garlic in a basin with the oil. Cook using microwaves only on high for 3 minutes. Heat the oven to 220 C. Add the pork, tomato purée, mace and marjoram to the onion and garlic. Mix in the wine and seasoning to taste. Make sure the ingredients are thoroughly combined in a moist mixture. Rinse and dry the chopped aubergine and mix it into the meat. Spoon the filling into the aubergine shells. Bake at 220 C using medium microwave setting for 12–15 minutes. Top each aubergine half with a little soured cream and sprinkle with sesame seeds.

PUFF-CRUST CAULIFLOWER

 HIGH

Combination:

 MEDIUM

 250 C

SERVES 4–6

◆ This is an original idea for turning a cauliflower into an unusual supper dish or vegetarian main dish. You can vary the cheese mixture, but retain the cream cheese base. Try adding some chopped nuts, chopped mushrooms or chopped cooked ham.

1 large cauliflower, trimmed
100 g/4 oz Cheddar cheese, grated
100 g/4 oz cream cheese
2 large tomatoès, peeled and finely chopped
1 small onion, grated
$\frac{1}{2}$ teaspoon dried or 1 teaspoon chopped
  fresh marjoram

2 tablespoons chopped parsley
salt and freshly ground black pepper
1 (370-g/13-oz) packet puff pastry
1 egg, beaten

Put the cauliflower in a large dish. Cover and cook using microwaves only on high for 5–7 minutes. Set aside until almost cold.

Beat the Cheddar into the cream cheese. Gradually beat in the tomato, onion and herbs, then add seasoning to taste. Roll out the pastry into a circle large enough to enclose the cauliflower completely. (Probably about 38–40 cm/15–16 in. in diameter). Spread the cheese mixture thickly in the middle of the pastry. Drain the cauliflower and place it upside down on top of the cheese mixture. Fold the pastry around the cauliflower. Trim off any excess pastry then brush the edges with a little beaten egg and seal firmly together. Place the cauliflower with the pastry joins underneath on a flan dish. Re-roll any pastry trimmings and cut out shapes to decorate the top of the pastry. Chill thoroughly. Meanwhile, heat the oven to 250 C.

Brush with beaten egg and bake the cauliflower at 250 C using medium microwave setting for 10 minutes, or until the pastry is well puffed and browned. Serve freshly cooked, cut into wedges.

SUPPER ONIONS

 HIGH

Combination:

 MEDIUM

 250 C

SERVES 4

◆ Slightly tangy Caerphilly cheese is ideal for this dish. Add chopped cooked ham or walnuts if you like.

4 large onions (Spanish, or of that size)
75 g/3 oz fresh breadcrumbs
75 g/3 oz Caerphilly cheese, crumbled
1 small carrot, coarsely grated

2 tablespoons chopped parsley
1 teaspoon rubbed sage
25 g/1 oz butter

Peel the onions, put them in a large casserole dish and cover. Alternatively, put the onions in a roasting bag and stand this in a flan dish, tucking the open end underneath one of the onions. Cook using microwaves only on high for 8–10 minutes, or until tender. Leave to cool until the onions can be handled. Heat the oven to 250 C.

Scoop the middles out of the onions, leaving a shell about two or three layers thick. The best way to do this is to cut into the middle of the onion using a sharp pointed knife, then use a teaspoon to scoop out the soft centre. Trim the hole at the top, enlarging and neatening it.

Chop the scooped-out onion and mix it with the remaining ingredients except for the butter. Stand the onion shells in a flan dish and press the mixture into them. Top each with a little butter and bake at 250 C using medium microwave setting for 6–8 minutes or until the filling is browned on top. Serve freshly cooked.

SOUFFLÉD VEGETABLE BAKE

 HIGH

Combination:

 MEDIUM

 250 C

SERVES 4–6

Illustrated on page 51

1 onion, chopped
175 g/6 oz carrots, sliced
25 g/1 oz butter or 2 tablespoons oil
350 g/12 oz white cabbage, shredded
1 (397-g/14-oz) can chopped tomatoes
1 (283-g/10-oz) can red kidney beans
salt and pepper
2 tablespoons chopped parsley

Topping
75 g/3 oz self-raising flour
salt and pepper
100 g/4 oz matured Cheddar cheese, grated
1 teaspoon dried or 1 tablespoon chopped fresh basil
4 eggs, separated
4 tablespoons milk

Place the onion and carrot in a large casserole dish with the butter or oil. Cover and cook using microwaves only on high for 5 minutes. Stir in the cabbage and tomatoes and re-cover the dish. Continue to cook on high for 5 minutes. Heat the oven to 250 C. Add the beans, seasoning and parsley to the vegetables. Stir well, then set aside.

For the topping, put the flour into a bowl and add a generous sprinkling of seasoning. Stir in the cheese and basil. Make a well in the middle of the dry ingredients and add the egg yolks. Stir the milk into the yolks, then gradually stir in the dry ingredients and beat thoroughly to eliminate any lumps of flour. Whisk the egg whites until they are stiff. Stir about a quarter of the egg whites into the mixture to soften it slightly. Use a metal spoon to fold the remaining egg white into the mixture. Take great care not to overmix and knock the air out. Spoon the topping over the vegetables, spreading it lightly to cover them completely.

Bake at 250 C and medium microwave setting for 12–15 minutes, or until the topping has risen, browned and slightly cracked. Serve at once.

VEGETABLE TIMBALE

 HIGH

Combination:

 MEDIUM

 250 C

SERVES 6

◆ This really is very tasty – vary the vegetables if you like but keep the mixture firm for success.

1 large aubergine, sliced
salt and freshly ground black pepper
225 g/8 oz carrots, thinly sliced
225 g/8 oz swede, cubed
225 g/8 oz potatoes, cubed

1 onion, chopped
100 g/4 oz Cheddar cheese, grated
100 g/4 oz fresh white breadcrumbs
2 eggs
knob of butter

Place the aubergine slices in a colander and sprinkle generously with salt. Leave over the sink or a bowl for 30 minutes, then rinse and dry well. Put the other vegetables in a large casserole dish and cover. Cook using microwaves only on high for 10–15 minutes or until tender. Mash the vegetables together, then press them through a sieve. Alternatively, cream the vegetables in a food processor.

Put the aubergine slices in a dish, cover and cook using microwaves only on high for 3 minutes. Heat the oven to 250 C. Beat the cheese, breadcrumbs and eggs into the mashed vegetables and add seasoning to taste. Grease an 18-cm/7-in deep round dish with butter. Lay half the aubergine slices overlapping in the bottom. Turn the vegetable mixture into the dish, top with the remaining aubergine slices and bake at 250 C using medium microwave setting for 10–15 minutes, or until browned. Leave in the dish for 15 minutes, then turn out and serve cut into wedges.

BEEFLESS BURGERS

 HIGH

Combination:

 MEDIUM

 250 C

SERVES 4

100 g/4 oz parsnips, grated
225 g/8 oz carrots, grated
225 g/8 oz swede, grated
1 large onion, finely chopped
25 g/1 oz butter, plus extra for cooking
100 g/4 oz fresh breadcrumbs

1 teaspoon chopped fresh thyme
1 teaspoon rubbed sage
4 tablespoons chopped parsley
salt and freshly ground black pepper
1 egg

Mix the vegetables in a casserole dish, add the butter and cover. Cook using microwaves only on high for 8 minutes. Heat the oven to 250 C.

Mix the vegetables well, then stir in the breadcrumbs, herbs, seasoning to taste and egg to bind. Divide the mixture into quarters and shape each portion into a big burger. Place on a well greased flan dish, pressing the burgers firmly into shape. Dot each one with a little butter and bake at 250 C using medium microwave setting for 15–20 minutes, or until the burgers are browned and cooked. Serve hot.

ALTERNATIVE METHOD
These also cook well on 250 C using high microwave setting for about 6–8 minutes.

Right *Pizza, (pages 64, 65) anti-clockwise from top, Prawn, Mushroom, Salami and Tomato*
Left *Lentil and Tomato Plait (page 66)*

SUPPER DISHES

CAULIFLOWER SPECIAL

 HIGH

Combination:

 MEDIUM

 220 C

SERVES 4

1 large cauliflower, trimmed
1 large onion, chopped
100 g/4 oz rindless bacon, chopped
100 g/4 oz button mushrooms, chopped
4 tomatoes, peeled and chopped
100 g/4 oz fresh breadcrumbs

50 g/2 oz cheese, grated
salt and freshly ground black pepper
2 tablespoons chopped parsley
½ teaspoon dried or 1 teaspoon chopped
  fresh thyme

Carefully scoop out the middle of the cauliflower, cutting the thick stalks neatly to leave a ring of florets all attached in the middle by the core. Chop the scooped out cauliflower and mix it with the onion in a large basin. Cover and cook using microwaves only on high for 5 minutes. Put the cauliflower shell in a large dish, cover and cook using microwaves only for 5 minutes. Heat the oven to 220 C.

Mix the remaining ingredients into the chopped cauliflower and onion. Press this mixture into the middle of the cauliflower shell and bake at 220 C using medium microwave setting for 12–15 minutes. Serve hot with a cheese or egg sauce (see page 120).

ALTERNATIVE METHOD
Cook at 220 C using high microwave setting for 8–10 minutes.

TOADS-IN-HOLES

Combination:

 MEDIUM

 250 C

SERVES 4

◆ Serve with an Onion sauce (see page 120) or with a Tomato sauce (see page 121). Alternatively make a salad to go with the toads-in-holes and forget about the gravy or sauce; tomatoes with onion or a creamy coleslaw are both suitable accompaniments.

450 g/1 lb sausages
100 g/4 oz plain flour
pinch of salt

2 eggs
300 ml/½ pint milk

Place the sausages in a 25-cm/10-in flan dish, arranging them to resemble the spokes of a wheel. Cook at 250 C using medium microwave setting for 5 minutes.

Put the flour and salt in a bowl. Make a well in the middle and add the eggs. Gradually beat in the milk, at the same time working in the flour to make a smooth batter.

Take the sausages from the oven and prick them to burst any bubbles of fat. Pour the batter into the dish and bake at 250 C using medium microwave setting for 15 minutes, or until the batter is browned and well risen. Serve at once, while still crisp and light.

ALTERNATIVE METHOD
This can also be cooked at 250 C using low microwave setting for 20–25 minutes.

VARIATION
Substitute 225 g/8 oz cooked ham, cubed, for the sausages. Do not cook separately first. Cook a finely chopped onion with a knob of butter using microwaves only on high for 2 minutes; add to the batter with ½ teaspoon dried mixed herbs. Put ham in greased dish with 100 g/4 oz sliced mushrooms. Pour in batter and cook as above.

TURNIP AND HAM GRATIN

 HIGH

Combination:

 MEDIUM

 250 C

SERVES 4

450 g/1 lb baby turnips, peeled and
    quartered
knob of butter
100 g/4 oz cooked ham, shredded
salt and freshly ground black pepper
150 ml/¼ pint milk or single cream
Topping
50 g/2 oz fresh breadcumbs

50 g/2 oz Caerphilly or Lancashire cheese,
    crumbled
4 spring onions, chopped
salt and freshly ground black pepper
25 g/1 oz butter or margarine

Place the turnip in a casserole dish with the butter. Cover and cook using microwaves only on high for 3 minutes. Rearrange the pieces of turnip in the dish, re-cover and cook on high for a further 3 minutes or until the turnip is about two-thirds cooked. Add the ham to the turnip, sprinkle in seasoning and pour in the milk or cream. Stir lightly to mix the ingredients.

    For the topping, mix the breadcrumbs with the cheese and spring onion. Add a little seasoning, then sprinkle the topping over the turnip mixture. Dot with the butter or margarine. Bake at 250 C and medium microwave setting for about 10 minutes, or until the topping has browned a little and the turnip is cooked.

    Serve freshly cooked, as an accompaniment or as a supper dish. Offer some warmed crusty bread with the gratin if you are serving it as a dish on its own. This also makes a tasty and unusual starter.

ALTERNATIVE METHOD
Turnip and ham gratin can also be cooked using a combination of high microwave setting and the grill. Preheat the grill. Prepare the dish exactly as in the recipe. Once assembled, cook the gratin under the grill using high microwave setting simultaneously for 5 minutes, or until the topping is browned.

CHICKEN LIVER SAVOURY

 HIGH

Combination:

 MEDIUM

 250 C

SERVES 4

1 large onion, chopped
1 large green pepper, deseeded and chopped
175 g/6 oz rindless bacon, chopped
salt and freshly ground black pepper
225 g/8 oz chicken livers, roughly chopped

175 g/6 oz mushrooms, sliced
4 large tomatoes, peeled and chopped
450 g/1 lb potatoes, thinly sliced
knob of butter

Put the onion, green pepper and bacon in a casserole dish. Cover and cook using microwaves only on high for 5 minutes. Stir in seasoning to taste, the chicken liver, mushroom and tomato. Put the sliced potato in a large basin or roasting bag and cover or loosely secure the open end of the bag. Cook using microwaves only on high for 8 minutes. Heat the oven to 250 C.

    Overlap the potato slices on top of the chicken liver mixture. Dot with butter and bake at 250 C using medium microwave setting for 15 minutes, or until well browned on top. Serve freshly cooked.

LEEK AND CHICKEN LOAF

 HIGH

Combination:

 MEDIUM

◆ 200 C

SERVES 4

350 g/12 oz leeks, halved lengthways and
   thinly sliced
225 g/8 oz carrots, grated
225 g/8 oz cooked chicken, minced or finely
   diced

75 g/3 oz fresh breadcrumbs
1 egg, beaten
salt and freshly ground black pepper

Make sure that the leeks are thoroughly washed and free of grit. Put them in a casserole dish, cover and cook using microwaves only on high for 8 minutes. Heat the oven to 200 C.

Mix all the remaining ingredients into the leeks, adding a generous amount of seasoning. Base-line and grease a 450-g/1-lb loaf dish, then press the mixture into it. Cook at 200 C using medium microwave setting for 15 minutes. Leave in the dish for 10 minutes, then turn out and serve cut into slices.

VARIATIONS
This tasty loaf can be used as a base for left-over turkey, pork or boiled ham as well as chicken. It also tastes good served cold, with mayonnaise flavoured with chopped fresh herbs.

PUMPKIN AND BACON BAKE

HIGH

Combination:

MEDIUM

◆ 200 C

SERVES 4

2 medium onions, chopped
225 g/8 oz rindless bacon, chopped
450 g/1 lb pumpkin, peeled and cut into chunks
salt and freshly ground black pepper
1 teaspoon dried marjoram

75 g/3 oz fresh breadcrumbs
75 g/3 oz Cheshire or Wensleydale cheese, crumbled
1 teaspoon mustard powder
25 g/1 oz butter or margarine

Put the onion and bacon in a casserole dish and cook using microwaves only on high for 5 minutes. Stir well and add the pumpkin cubes. Cover the dish and cook on high for a further 4 minutes. Stir in the seasoning to taste and the marjoram.

Mix the breadcrumbs with the cheese and mustard. Add a little seasoning and sprinkle the mixture lightly over the pumpkin. Dot with the butter or margarine and bake at 200 C using medium microwave power for 15 minutes, or until the pumpkin is tender and the topping browned. Serve piping hot.

VARIATION
This bake is also good for marrow or courgettes – if you want to add some colour to these vegetables, then mix in some diced swede or carrot.

PIZZA

HIGH

Combination:

 MEDIUM

 250 C

SERVES 2—4

Illustrated on page 59

◆ The combination of microwaves and conventional heat cooks pizza very well, producing results which are moist and light as well as crisp and golden round the edges. I find that a round dish made of ovenproof glassware gives the best results, for if the base of the dish is too thick and heavy the middle of the pizza can be slightly soggy.

Base
100 g/4 oz strong white flour
salt and freshly ground black pepper
2 teaspoons easy-blend dried yeast or ordinary dried yeast
50 ml/2 fl oz lukewarm water
1 tablespoon oil
Topping
1 large onion, chopped

1 tablespoon oil
2 cloves garlic, crushed
½ teaspoon dried marjoram
350 g/12 oz tomatoes
1 tablespoon capers, roughly chopped (optional)
salt and freshly ground black pepper
175 g/6 oz mozzarella cheese, cubed
10—12 black olives, stoned

Put the flour in a bowl and add a pinch of salt. Stir in the easy-blend dried yeast. If using ordinary dried yeast, then sprinkle it over the lukewarm water and leave in a warm place until the yeast has dissolved and the liquid is frothy. Add the oil and water or yeast liquid to the flour and mix together to make a soft dough.

Turn the dough out on to a lightly floured surface and knead thoroughly until very smooth and elastic. Lightly flour the bowl, put the dough in it and cover with a damp cloth or a piece of cling film. Leave in a warm place until doubled in size.

Meanwhile, prepare the topping: put the onion, oil and garlic in a basin and cook using microwaves only on high for 3 minutes. Stir in the marjoram. Peel the tomatoes if you like – to do this put them in a bowl and cover with boiling water, leave for 30—60 seconds, then drain and peel. Slice the tomatoes.

Lightly grease a 25-cm/10-in flan dish. Turn the risen dough out on to a lightly floured surface and knead it very briefly. Roll it out into a circle to fit the base of the dish. Lift the dough into the dish, pressing it into the corners but not up the sides. Spread the onion mixture evenly over the dough, then top with the tomato slices and sprinkle with capers (if used). Season with a little salt and plenty of pepper. Top with the mozzarella and olives, distributing both evenly over the pizza.

Bake the pizza at 250 C using medium microwave setting for 10—12 minutes, or until the top is bubbling and lightly browned and the edges are brown and crisp. Serve freshly cooked, with a green salad.

TOPPING IDEAS FOR PIZZA
The great thing about pizza is that you can use all sorts of different ingredients to create a kaleidoscope of flavours and colours. Opt for generous portions of one or two ingredients or give licence to your imagination in combining several favourite foods. Each of the following toppings is to go over the basic onion, garlic and marjoram mixture used in the main recipe.

Mushroom Pizza Add 225 g/8 oz thinly sliced button mushrooms and top with the mozzarella as in the main recipe. Sprinkle with a little chopped parsley – if you like – before serving.

No-cheese Pizza Add 175 g/6 oz thinly sliced button mushrooms and 100 g/4 oz thinly sliced tomatoes. Sprinkle a little olive oil and some chopped black olives over the top before cooking. Add a little chopped fresh basil or parsley before serving.

Mixed Vegetable Pizza Add 1 chopped green pepper to the onion mixture before cooking. Top with canned artichoke hearts, a few sliced button mushrooms, 1 small sliced courgette and 100 g/4 oz thinly sliced tomatoes. You will be clever to balance any more than 100 g/4 oz thinly sliced mozzarella cheese on top!

Prawn Pizza Top with 175 g/6 oz frozen peeled cooked prawns, 100 g/4 oz chopped tomatoes, the cheese and olives as in the main recipe.

Spicy-hot Pepper and Corn Pizza A good one for chilli-lovers! Add 1 or 2 chopped green chillies (depending on how much you love them) to the onion mixture before cooking. Top the pizza with 100 g/4 oz chopped cooked ham or lean bacon and 75 g/3 oz sweetcorn. Add the 175 g/6 oz mozzarella cheese but omit the olives. (Pickled jalepeno chillies taste particularly good, but don't cook them with the onion, just add them on top.)

Salami and Tomato Pizza Top with 100 g/4 oz salami, then add the tomatoes and mozzarella with olives as in the main recipe.

Bacon and Pepper Pizza Add 2 chopped green or red peppers to the onion mixture before cooking. Chop 225 g/8 oz lean bacon and sprinkle it over the pizza. Top with 100 g/4 oz chopped tomatoes and 100 g/4 oz diced mozzarella.

Tuna and Tomato Pizza Add 1 (198-g/7-oz) can tuna, drained and flaked, and 225 g/8 oz chopped tomatoes. Top with the mozzarella and olives as in the main recipe.

CALZONE

Combination:

 MEDIUM

◆ 250 C

SERVES 2

◆ Calzone is a traditional Italian speciality – a sort of folded-over pizza. This is good and filling – for those with lighter appetites four may share!

225 g/8 oz strong white flour
1 sachet easy-blend yeast, or 3 teaspoons
   ordinary dried yeast
$\frac{1}{4}$ teaspoon salt
150 ml/$\frac{1}{4}$ pint lukewarm water
2 tablespoons oil
Filling
50 g/2 oz salami, thinly sliced

225 g/8 oz tomatoes, thickly sliced
3 cloves garlic, finely chopped
generous pinch of dried marjoram
225 g/8 oz mozzarella cheese, sliced
salt and freshly ground black pepper

Put the flour in a bowl and mix in the easy-blend yeast and salt. If using ordinary dried yeast, then sprinkle it over the water and leave in a warm place until dissolved and frothy. Make a well in the flour and pour in the water or yeast liquid and the oil. Mix into a soft dough, then knead thoroughly for about 10 minutes, until smooth and very elastic. Put in a floured bowl, cover with a damp cloth or cling film and leave in a warm place until doubled in size.

Turn the dough on to a lightly floured surface and knead briefly. Roll into an oblong shape measuring about 40 cm/16 in. in length. When folded in half the calzone must fit into a 25-cm/10-in flan dish.

Arrange the filling ingredients on one half of the dough, seasoning well. Fold the other half over and pinch the edges of the dough together to seal in the filling. Lift on to a large greased flan dish and leave in a warm place for 20–30 minutes. Meanwhile, heat the oven to 250 C.

Bake the calzone at 250 C using medium microwave setting for 10–12 minutes, or until browned and crisp. Serve freshly cooked.

SAVOURY CHARLOTTE

Combination:

◈ MEDIUM

◆ 220 C

SERVES 2

1 tablespoon prepared mustard
75 g/3 oz butter
6 slices bread (crusts removed if you like)
100 g/4 oz matured Cheddar cheese, grated
4 tablespoons snipped chives or chopped
   spring onions

2 eggs
300 ml/½ pint milk
salt and freshly ground black pepper

Cream the mustard and butter together, then spread the mixture on the bread. Cut the slices into triangles. Lightly grease a small soufflé or casserole dish. Layer the bread with the cheese and chives or spring onion in the prepared dish. Beat the eggs with the milk, adding a little seasoning. Pour this mixture over the bread and leave to soak for at least 15 minutes.

Bake the charlotte at 220 C using medium microwave setting for 15 minutes, or until crisp and golden. Serve immediately – this tastes good with a tomato salad.

LENTIL AND TOMATO PLAIT

◈ HIGH

Combination:

◈ MEDIUM

◆ 250 C

SERVES 6

Illustrated on page 59

◆ Very often recipes rich in wholefoods are set aside as alternatives for non-meat eaters – but do try this, it's full of flavour and delicious with a creamy vegetable dish such as leeks in cheese sauce.

100 g/4 oz lentils
1 onion, chopped
300 ml/½ pint boiling water
225 g/8 oz plain wholemeal flour
150 g/5 oz margarine
4 tablespoons water

225 g/8 oz tomatoes, peeled and chopped
100 g/4 oz mozzarella cheese, diced
salt and freshly ground black pepper
1 egg, beaten
2 teaspoons sesame seeds

Put the lentils, onion and water in a casserole dish. Cover and cook using microwaves only on high for 10 minutes. Heat the oven to 250 C.

Meanwhile make the pastry: put the flour in a bowl and rub in the margarine until the mixture resembles fine breadcrumbs. Stir in the water to bind the ingredients together. Press the pastry into a ball using your fingertips.

Add the tomato, mozzarella and seasoning to the lentils. Mix well. Roll out the pastry into an oblong measuring about 25 × 30 cm/12 × 10 in. If you have an oven with a turntable, then remember that you are going to have to fit the plait on to a flan dish measuring about 25 cm/10 in. in diameter.

Pile the lentil mixture down the middle of the pastry. Brush the edges of the pastry with a little beaten egg. Make cuts into the pastry, from the edge towards the filling, at intervals of about 2.5 cm/1 in. Fold the strips of pastry over the filling, crossing them over from alternate sides. Press the edges well to seal in the filling. Lift the plait on to a large flan dish and brush with beaten egg. Sprinkle the sesame seeds over the pastry and bake at 250 C using medium microwave setting for 12–15 minutes, or until well browned and cooked through.

Serve hot, cut into thick slices. A salad accompaniment is ideal.

Top *Almond-crusted Apricot Pie (page 77)*
Bottom *Lamb Cutlets en Croûte (page 69)*

SAVOURY AND SWEET PASTRY RECIPES ◆

SMOKED COD AND CORN QUICHE

 HIGH

Combination:

 MEDIUM

◆ **220 C**

SERVES 6

◆ The ingredients and method given in this recipe for making Shortcrust Pastry are referred to as **1 quantity Shortcrust Pastry** in other recipes that call for shortcrust pastry.

Shortcrust Pastry
175 g/6 oz plain flour
salt and freshly ground black pepper
75 g/3 oz margarine (or 40 g/1½ oz margarine and 40 g/1½ oz lard)
2 tablespoons water

Filling
225 g/8 oz frozen sweetcorn
450 g/1 lb smoked cod (or haddock) fillet
2 tablespoons snipped chives
3 eggs
300 ml/½ pint milk or single cream
salt and freshly ground black pepper

To make the pastry, put the flour into a bowl and add a pinch of salt. Add the fat, cut it into pieces and rub it into the flour until the mixture resembles fine breadcrumbs. Mix in the water to make a short dough, pressing it together with the fingertips.

On a lightly floured surface, roll out the pastry into a circle large enough to line a 25-cm/10-in flan dish. Roll the rolling pin over the rim of the dish to remove the excess pastry and prick the base all over. Chill the pastry case briefly.

Put the frozen sweetcorn in a basin and cook using microwaves only on high for 4 minutes. Bake the empty pastry case at 220 C and medium microwave setting for 5 minutes. Skin the fish and cut it into small cubes. Sprinkle the sweetcorn and fish over the base of the flan case. Top with the chives. Beat the eggs with the milk or cream and add seasoning to taste. Pour the egg mixture into the flan case and bake at 220 C using medium microwave setting for 18–20 minutes, or until golden.

CORNISH PASTIES

Combination:

 MEDIUM

 220 C

MAKES 4

1½ quantity Shortcrust Pastry (above)
Filling
225 g/8 oz minced beef
1 small onion, chopped
100 g/4 oz carrots, diced

100 g/4 oz potatoes, diced
dash of Worcestershire sauce
2 tablespoons water
salt and freshly ground black pepper
beaten egg to glaze

Cut the pastry into quarters. Prepare the filling: mix the beef with the vegetables and a generous dash of Worcestershire sauce. Add the water and plenty of seasoning and make sure all the ingredients are well mixed. Heat the oven to 220 C.

Roll out the pastry quarters on a lightly floured surface to give four 18-cm/7-in circles. Divide the filling between the circles and brush the edges of the pastry with a little water. Fold both sides of the pastry up over the filling to meet in the middle and form a pastie shape. Pinch the edges together firmly, making a neat join and leaving a small gap in the middle for the steam to escape. Place the pasties on two flat round dishes – flan dishes are ideal. Brush with a little beaten egg and bake at 220 C using medium microwave setting. Put one dish on the turntable and the second dish on the wire rack above. Bake for 12 minutes, then swop the dishes. Cook for a further 6–8 minutes, or until the pasties are browned. Serve freshly baked or transfer the pasties to a wire rack to cool. They taste good warm or cold.

STEAK AND KIDNEY PIE

 MEDIUM

Combination:

 MEDIUM

 220 C

SERVES 4

◆ If you use stewing steak, or a cut that calls for lengthy, traditional cooking, then you can always stew the steak and kidney filling by a conventional method.

450 g/1 lb good-quality, lean braising steak, diced
225 g/8 oz ox kidney, diced
1 onion, finely chopped
salt and freshly ground black pepper
2 tablespoons plain flour
bay leaf
1 teaspoon dried thyme
about 150 ml/$\frac{1}{4}$ pint boiling water
1 quantity Shortcrust Pastry (page 68)

Make sure that the meat is trimmed of any gristle. It is best cut into small pieces across the grain. Mix the steak, kidney, onion and plenty of seasoning with the flour. Place in a pie dish and add the herbs. Pour in enough boiling water to come just to the top of the meat without covering it. Cover the dish with a plate or microwave cling film and cook using microwaves only on medium for 10 minutes. Stir well, then cook for a further 10 minutes. Set aside for 15 minutes. Heat the oven to 220 C.

On a lightly floured board roll out the pastry into a piece large enough to cover the pie with about 2.5 cm/1 in extra. Cut a narrow strip from the edge of the pastry. Dampen the rim of the dish and stick the pastry strip on it. Dampen the pastry edge, then lift the lid over the pie and press the edges firmly to seal in the filling. Trim off the excess pastry. Holding your finger on the top edge of the pie, tap the edge of the pastry all round with the blunt edge of a knife. Pinch the edge into decorative scallops and brush the top of the pie with egg.

Bake at 220 C using medium microwave setting for 15 minutes, or until well browned on top and cooked through. Serve piping hot.

LAMB CUTLETS EN CROÛTE

 HIGH

Combination:

 MEDIUM

 250 C

SERVES 4

Illustrated on page 67

◆ For the preparation of courgettes with mushrooms, in our picture, see page 115.

100 g/4 oz frozen chopped spinach
50 g/2 oz rindless lean bacon, finely chopped
50 g/2 oz button mushrooms, finely chopped
50 g/2 oz fresh breadcrumbs
salt and freshly ground black pepper
4 fairly thin lamb cutlets
1 (370-g/13-oz) packet puff pastry, defrosted if frozen
1 egg, beaten

Put the spinach in a basin and heat using microwaves only on high for 1–2 minutes, or until soft. Heat the oven to 250 C. Stir the bacon, mushroom, breadcrumbs and seasoning into the spinach. Trim excess fat off the cutlets and clean the ends of the bones of all meat. Roll out the pastry on a lightly floured surface into a thick oblong measuring 25 × 50 cm/10 × 20 in. Cut in half to make two squares, then cut these in half diagonally into two triangles. Place some of the stuffing in the middle of each triangle. Lay a lamb cutlet on top, with the bone arranged beyond the edge of the pastry. Lift the pastry corners over the cutlets and trim off any excess. Brush the edges of the pastry with a little beaten egg and press them in place to seal in the filling.

Re-roll the pastry trimmings and cut out leaves to decorate the pastry cases. Turn the cutlets over so that the pastry joins are underneath. Put the pastry leaves on top and brush with beaten egg. Place on a flan dish and bake at 250 C using medium microwave setting for 12–15 minutes.

Place cutlet frills on the bone ends before serving freshly cooked.

PORK AND SPINACH PIE

 HIGH

Combination:

 MEDIUM

 200 C

SERVES 4

1 large onion, chopped
1 clove garlic, crushed
1 green pepper, deseeded and chopped
small knob of butter
225 g/8 oz frozen spinach
1 teaspoon rubbed sage

salt and freshly ground black pepper
a little freshly grated nutmeg
450 g/1 lb minced pork
150 ml/¼ pint dry cider or water
1 quantity Shortcrust Pastry (page 68)
beaten egg to glaze

Place the onion in a pie dish with the garlic, green pepper and butter. Cover with a plate or microwave cling film and cook using microwaves only on high for 3 minutes. Add the spinach, re-cover and cook for 5 minutes. Heat the oven to 200 C.

Stir the sage, seasoning and nutmeg into the vegetable mixture. Add the minced pork and mix it in thoroughly. Mix in the cider or water. Roll out the pastry large enough to cover the top of the pie dish with about 2.5 cm/1 in extra. Trim a narrow strip from the edge of the pastry. Dampen the edge of the dish and press the pastry strip on to it. Brush the pastry rim with a little water. Lift the main piece of pastry over the top and press the edges together to seal in the filling. Trim off any excess pastry and re-roll to make decorative trimmings for the top of the pie. Brush these with a little water and press on top. Brush the pie with a little beaten egg and bake at 200 C using medium microwave setting for 20 minutes, or until browned. Serve hot, with potatoes and a moist vegetable dish like ratatouille.

ALTERNATIVE METHOD
If using low microwave setting with 200 C, then allow 25–30 minutes cooking time.

SAVOURY ROLY-POLY

 HIGH

Combination:

 MEDIUM

 200 C

SERVES 4–6

1 large onion, chopped
225 g/8 oz rindless bacon, roughly chopped
100 g/4 oz mushrooms, sliced
2 tomatoes, peeled and chopped
2 tablespoons chopped parsley
salt and freshly ground black pepper

Pastry
225 g/8 oz self-raising flour
100 g/4 oz shredded suet
salt
150 ml/¼ pint water

Put the onion and bacon in a basin and cook using microwaves only on high for 5 minutes. Stir in the mushroom, tomato, parsley and seasoning to taste. Heat the oven to 200 C.

Put the flour in a bowl and mix in the suet. Add a pinch of salt, then mix in the water to make a soft pastry dough. Turn it out on to a lightly floured surface and knead it quickly together into a smooth ball. Roll out into an oblong measuring 23 × 33 cm/9 × 12 in. Spread the filling over the pastry, leaving the edges free. Roll up from the short side and pinch the pastry edge to seal in the filling.

Lift the roly-poly on to a large flan dish and bake at 200 C using medium microwave setting for 15–17 minutes, or until the pastry is risen, browned and cooked through. Serve piping hot, cut into thick slices.

STILTON PEAR FLAN

 HIGH

Combination:

 MEDIUM

◆ 250 C

SERVES 6

◆ A slightly weird combination of ingredients makes up a mouthwatering filling for this flan.

1 quantity Shortcrust Pastry (page 68)
Filling
225 g/8 oz leeks, halved and sliced
knob of butter
4 pears (select fruit which is just ripe but not too soft)

a little lemon juice
225 g/8 oz Stilton cheese, crumbled
salt and freshly ground black pepper
3 tablespoons double cream (or use single cream; milk can be used for a not-quite-as-delicious result)

Roll out the pastry and use to line a 23-cm/9-in flan dish. Prick the base and chill for 10 minutes. Make sure that the leeks are thoroughly washed and free of all grit. Put in a large basin or casserole dish with the butter and cover. Cook using microwaves only on high for 7 minutes. Heat the oven to 250 C.

Place a piece of greaseproof paper in the pastry case and sprinkle in a handful of baking beans or dried peas. Bake at 250 C using medium microwave setting for 5 minutes. Remove the paper and beans, then continue to cook for a further 3 minutes, or until the pastry is cooked.

Peel, core and roughly chop the pears, then sprinkle with lemon juice to prevent discoloration. Mix most of the cheese into the leeks. Add seasoning, the chopped pears and the cream. Turn this filling into the pastry case and sprinkle the rest of the cheese on top. Bake at 250 C using medium microwave setting for 3–5 minutes. Serve immediately – delicious!

QUICHE LORRAINE

 HIGH

Combination:

 MEDIUM

 250/200 C

SERVES 6

1 quantity Shortcrust Pastry (page 68)
Filling
2 onions, chopped
175 g/6 oz rindless bacon, roughly chopped

100 g/4 oz Emmental cheese
3 eggs
300 ml/½ pint single cream or milk
salt and freshly ground black pepper

Turn the pastry out on to a lightly floured surface and roll out into a circle large enough to line a 25-cm/10-in flan dish. Lift the pastry into the dish and trim off any excess by rolling the rolling pin over the edge of the dish. Prick the base all over, then chill lightly. For the filling, put the onion and bacon in a basin and cook using microwaves only on high for 5 minutes.

When the pastry has chilled for about 15–20 minutes, bake it at 250 C (without preheating the oven) using medium microwave setting for 5 minutes. Remove from the oven and re-set the temperature to 200 C.

Sprinkle the onion and bacon mixture into the quiche, then add the cheese. Beat the eggs with the cream or milk and add seasoning to taste. Pour this mixture into the quiche and bake at 250 C using medium microwave setting for 12–15 minutes, or until the quiche is lightly browned. Serve hot or warm.

ALTERNATIVE METHOD
Bake the empty pastry shell at 250 C using low microwave setting for 8 minutes. Allow about 15–18 minutes with the filling, at 200 C using low microwave setting.

VOL-AU-VENT CASE

Combination:

 MEDIUM

◆ 250 C

SERVES 4

1 (370-g/13-oz) packet puff pastry
1 egg, beaten

Cut the pastry in half. Roll out each half into a 20-cm/8-in circle. Use a plate as a guide for trimming the edges neatly. From the middle of one pastry circle cut a 14-cm/5½-in circle. Lift out the small circle: this forms the lid of the vol-au-vent. The pastry ring forms the side of the vol-au-vent.

Place the large circle of pastry on a flan dish. Dampen the pastry ring and lift it on top of the large circle, pressing it neatly all round the edge. Prick the middle of the vol-au-vent, then chill thoroughly. Chill the lid too. Heat the oven to 250 C.

Brush the top of the lid and the top of the ring of pastry with a little beaten egg. Take care not to spill egg down the sides of the pastry or it will not rise evenly. Put the vol-au-vent case on the wire rack and the lid straight on the turntable. Bake at 250 C using medium microwave setting for 4–5 minutes. The case should be cooked, so take it from the oven and transfer to a wire rack to cool. Transfer the lid to the rack and cook for a further 1½–2 minutes, or until puffed and browned.

The case can be used for sweet or savoury fillings, and served hot or cold.

VOL-AU-VENT FILLINGS
Seafood Make 300 ml/½ pint Béchamel Sauce (see page 120). Mix in 100 g/4 oz peeled cooked prawns, 225 g/8 oz white fish (uncooked, but skinned and cubed), 2 tablespoons chopped parsley, grated rind of ½ lemon and seasoning to taste.
Chicken Make 300 ml/½ pint mushroom sauce (see page 120). Add 225 g/8 oz chopped cooked chicken and 2 tablespoons chopped parsley. Taste for seasoning and cook for 2 minutes, then spoon the mixture into the case. Serve hot.

SAUSAGE ROLL SPECIALS

Combination:

 MEDIUM

◆ 250 C

MAKES 10

1 large onion, chopped
2 rashers rindless bacon, chopped
450 g/1 lb sausagemeat
salt and freshly ground black pepper

1 teaspoon rubbed sage
½ teaspoon dried thyme
1 (370-g/13-oz) packet puff pastry
1 egg, beaten

Heat the oven to 250 C. Mix all the ingredients apart from the pastry and egg. On a lightly floured surface roll out the pastry into an oblong measuring about 28 × 33 cm/11 × 13 in. Divide the sausagemeat mixture in half and form both pieces into long rolls, about 33 cm/13 in. in length. Place the rolls on the pastry and cut it down the middle. Brush the edges with a little beaten egg, then fold them over and seal. Cut each long roll into five pieces and brush with beaten egg.

Place the sausage rolls on two flan dishes. Put one flan dish on the turntable, the other on the rack and bake at 250 C using medium microwave setting for 10 minutes, or until the top batch is puffed and well browned. Remove from the oven and move the lower dish up on to the rack. Continue cooking for a further 2–3 minutes. Cool the sausage rolls on a wire rack. Serve warm or cold.

CHEESE AND SPINACH PIES

◈ HIGH

Combination:

◈ MEDIUM

◆ 250 C

MAKES 8

100 g/4 oz frozen chopped spinach
1 small onion, finely chopped
225 g/8 oz feta cheese, crumbled
pinch of oregano

salt and freshly ground black pepper
1 (250-g/8.¾-oz) packet puff pastry, defrosted
   if frozen
1 egg, beaten

Heat the oven to 250 C. Put the spinach in a large basin and heat using microwaves only on high for 2–3 minutes, or until defrosted. Add the onion, cheese and oregano and mix thoroughly. Sprinkle in a little seasoning but do not overdo it.

On a lightly floured surface, roll out the pastry into an oblong measuring 50 × 25 cm/20 × 10 in. Cut into eight squares. Divide the spinach mixture between the pastry squares and brush the edges of the pastry with beaten egg. Fold the corners over the filling to make neat triangles, pressing the pastry together well to seal in the filling. Put four triangles on each of two large, flat round dishes and brush with beaten egg.

Bake at 250 C using medium microwave setting, on two levels, for 7 minutes. The pies on the top level should be well puffed and golden. If not then cook for a little longer. Remove the cooked pies from the oven, lift the dish from the turntable up on to the higher level and cook for a further 3 minutes, or until the pies are puffed and browned. Cool the pies on a wire rack. They can be served hot, warm or cold.

MINCEMEAT FLAN

Combination:

 MEDIUM

◆ 220 C

SERVES 6–8

1½ quantity Shortcrust Pastry (page 68)
450 g/1 lb mincemeat
grated rind of 1 orange

2 tablespoons rum
milk to glaze

Heat the oven to 220 C. On a lightly floured surface, roll out two-thirds of the pastry and use to line a 20-cm/8-in flan dish.

Mix the mincemeat with the orange rind and rum, then spread the mixture in the flan case. Roll the remaining pastry into a 20-cm/8-in square and cut into narrow strips. Dampen the pastry edge of the flan, then arrange the strips in a lattice pattern over the filling, pressing the pastry edges together firmly to keep the strips in place.

Brush the lattice with a little milk and bake at 220 C using medium microwave setting for 10–12 minutes. Serve hot or cold, with custard, brandy sauce or cream.

VARIATION
If you really want to make this a bit different, then flavour the pastry with the grated rind of 1 orange and add 50 g/2 oz ground almonds before mixing in the water.

APPLE PIE

Combination:

 MEDIUM

 200 C

SERVES 4–6

◆ Follow this recipe as a basic guide to cooking your own favourite fruit pies. If the fruit requires lengthy cooking, then start by cooking it alone using microwaves only for a few minutes, just to soften it. You will find this method successful with gooseberries and blackcurrants, for example.

1 quantity Shortcrust Pastry (page 68)
675 g/1½ lb cooking apples, peeled, cored and
  sliced

100 g/4 oz sugar
4 cloves
milk to glaze

Heat the oven to 200 C. On a lightly floured surface, roll out the dough into a piece about 3.5 cm/1½ in larger than the top of the pie dish. Cut a thin strip from the edge of the pastry. Dampen the rim of the dish and press the strip of pastry on to it. Dampen the pastry lightly. Fill the dish with the apples, sprinkling in the sugar between the layers. Add the cloves and lift the pastry lid over the top. Press the pastry edges together, then trim off the excess. Use the blunt side of a knife blade to tap the pastry edges together, at the same time pressing your finger lightly on top of the pastry to hold the edge out. Pinch the pastry edges into decorative scallops and brush the top with a little milk.

Bake the pie at 200 C using medium microwave setting for 15 minutes, or until golden brown and cooked. Serve hot, with cream or custard.

VARIATIONS

Apple Pie Plus Cheer up a simple apple pie by adding some raisins, grated orange rind, a sliced banana or two, canned peach slices, chopped preserved stem ginger or canned pineapple chunks.

Blackberry Pie Follow the main recipe using 450 g/1 lb fresh or frozen blackberries instead of the apple. You may like to combine blackberries and apples in the pie.

Pear Pie Peel, core and quarter about 450 g/1 lb ripe, firm pears. (The exact quantity will depend on the size of the dish.) Cut down the quantity of sugar to 50 g/2 oz and add 2 tablespoons chopped preserved ginger or crystallised ginger. Serve the pie with soured cream.

ALTERNATIVE METHOD

Using 200 C and low microwave setting, allow about 15 minutes cooking time for the apple pie.

ALMOND-CRUSTED APRICOT PIE

 HIGH

Combination:

 MEDIUM

 220 C

SERVES 4–6

Illustrated on page 67

◆ Try dried peaches or pears, or a combination of both, instead of the apricots in this pie.

Almond Pastry
100 g/4 oz plain flour
50 g/2 oz butter
50 g/2 oz ground almonds
25 g/1 oz sugar
2 tablespoons water
egg white to brush

caster sugar to dust
Filling
250 ml/8 fl oz orange juice
50 g/2 oz demerara sugar
1 teaspoon cinnamon
450 g/1 lb no-need-to-soak dried apricots

Put the flour in a bowl and rub in the butter until the mixture resembles fine breadcrumbs. Stir in the almonds and sugar, then mix in the water to make a soft pastry dough. Press together with the fingertips and shape into a ball. Wrap in plastic and chill while preparing the filling.

Mix the orange juice with the sugar and cinnamon in a basin. Heat using microwaves only on high for 2 minutes. Stir well. Put the apricots in a pie dish and pour in the orange juice mixture. Heat the oven to 220 C.

Roll out the pastry on a lightly floured surface to about 5 cm/2 in larger than the top of the dish. Cut a narrow strip from the edge of the pastry. Dampen the edge of the dish and press the pastry strip on to it. Lift the pastry over the pie and press the edges down firmly to seal in the filling. Trim off the excess pastry and tap the edges together with the blunt edge of a knife. At the same time, push the edge of the pastry down from the top to hold it in place. Pinch the edges into a scalloped pattern and re-roll the trimmings. Cut out decorative shapes and stick them on top of the pie with a little water. Brush the pie with a little egg white and sprinkle with caster sugar. Bake at 220 C using medium microwave setting for 10 minutes, or until the pie is browned on top. Serve hot or warm with double cream.

APPLE TURNOVERS

Combination:

 MEDIUM

 250 C

MAKES 6

350 g/12 oz cooking apples, peeled, cored and chopped
a little lemon juice
25 g/1 oz sugar
generous pinch of ground cloves

flour to dust
1 (250-g/8¾-oz) packet puff pastry, defrosted if frozen
1 egg white, lightly whisked
caster sugar to dust

Mix the apples with lemon juice to prevent discoloration, then stir in the sugar and ground cloves. Heat the oven to 250 C. On a lightly floured surface, roll out the pastry to an oblong measuring slightly larger than 38 × 25 cm/15 × 10 in. Trim the edges and cut into six 13-cm/5-in squares. Divide the apple mixture between the squares and brush the pastry edges with a little egg white. Fold the pastry over the filling to make triangles, pressing the edges together firmly. Put the turnovers on two flan dishes and brush with egg white. Sprinkle with caster sugar, then place one dish straight on the turntable, the second on the wire rack above.

Bake at 250 C using medium microwave setting for 7 minutes. Remove the top dish from the oven and move the lower dish up on to the rack. Cook for a further 3 minutes. The turnovers should be well puffed and golden. Cool on a wire rack – these taste superb when warm.

PUMPKIN PIE

 HIGH

Combination:

 MEDIUM

 250/200 C

SERVES 6–8

675 g/1½ lb pumpkin, peeled and cubed
1 quantity Shortcrust Pastry (page 68)
1 teaspoon cinnamon
1 teaspoon ground ginger
½ teaspoon grated nutmeg

100 g/4 oz sugar
4 tablespoons sherry
300 ml/½ pint single cream
4 eggs, beaten

Put the pumpkin cubes in a large casserole dish or roasting bag. Cover the dish or loosely close the bag with a plastic tie or rubber band. Cook using microwaves only on high for 13–15 minutes, or until tender. Roll out the pastry on a lightly floured surface into a circle large enough to line a 25-cm/10-in flan dish. Trim the excess pastry off by rolling the rolling pin over the rim of the dish. Prick the pastry all over and chill. Cook the chilled pastry case at 250 C using medium microwave setting for 5 minutes. Remove the pastry case and reduce the oven heat to 200 C.

Purée the cooked pumpkin in a blender or by pressing it through a sieve. Beat in the spices, sugar, sherry, cream and eggs. When thoroughly combined, pour the mixture into the flan case and bake at 200 C using medium microwave setting for 15 minutes. The filling should be set, slightly risen and lightly browned.

Serve the pumpkin pie warm, with double cream.

ECCLES PUFFS

Combination:

 MEDIUM

 250 C

MAKES 12

◆ These are not quite what you would expect of Eccles cakes but they do taste good!

50 g/2 oz currants
1 tablespoon soft brown sugar
grated rind of ½ orange
grated rind of ½ lemon
25 g/1 oz mixed peel

knob of butter
1 (250-g/8¾-oz) packet puff pastry
1 egg white
caster sugar to dust

Heat the oven to 250 C. Mix the currants with the sugar, fruit rinds and peel. Add a small knob of butter to bind the mixture.

Roll out the pastry into a 30-cm/12-in square. Cut out 24 5-cm/2-in circles. Divide the filling between half the circles. Brush the edges of the pastry with a little egg white, then press a second circle on top. Very lightly roll out the circles as thinly as possible without allowing the filling to break through. Make three slits in the top of each.

Place the filled circles on two flan dishes and brush with a little egg white. Sprinkle with caster sugar and bake at 250 C using medium microwave setting. Place one dish of Eccles puffs on the turntable and the second on the rack above. Remove the top dish after 5 minutes, when the little pastries should be well puffed and golden. Move the lower dish up and cook for a further 2 minutes. Transfer to a wire rack to cool. These taste very morish when warm.

Breads, clockwise from top, Soda Bread (page 81),
Currant Buns (page 85), Basic Bread,
white and wholemeal (page 80), Milk Loaf (page 81)

BREADS AND
SCONES

BASIC BREAD

Combination:

 MEDIUM

◆ 250 C

**MAKES 1 LARGE
LOAF OR 2 SMALL
LOAVES**

Illustrated on page 79

450 g/1 lb strong white or wholemeal flour
1 teaspoon salt
1 teaspoon sugar
50 g/2 oz margarine

1 sachet easy-blend dried yeast or 3
teaspoons ordinary dried yeast
300 ml/½ pint lukewarm water

Line a 1-kg/2-lb loaf dish with greaseproof paper and grease the paper thoroughly. The paper should stand above the rim of the dish by 2.5 cm/1 in, but it should not be too high.

Place the flour, salt and sugar in a bowl. Rub in the margarine and stir in the easy-blend yeast. If using ordinary dried yeast, then sprinkle it over the lukewarm water and leave in a warm place until the yeast has dissolved and the mixture is frothy.

Make a well in the dry ingredients and pour in the water or yeast liquid. Gradually stir in the flour to make a stiff dough. Use your hand to mix the last of the flour into the dough. Turn the dough out on to a lightly floured surface and knead it until very smooth and elastic. This first kneading should take about 10 minutes. Lightly flour the bowl and put the dough back into it. Cover with a damp cloth or a piece of cling film and leave in a warm place until doubled in size.

Turn the risen dough out on to a lightly floured surface and knead it briefly to knock out the gas. Press the dough into the prepared dish and cover with a dampened cloth or a piece of cling film. Leave in a warm place until the dough is well risen – it should stand above the rim of the dish.

Brush the dough with a little water and bake at 250 C using medium microwave setting for 10–12 minutes or until the loaf is browned on top. Leave in the dish for a few minutes, then turn the bread out on to a wire rack to cool and remove the paper. The base of the bread will not be brown, but the top should be brown and crusty and, of course, the loaf should be cooked through.

NOTE
This recipe gives the basic technique for making dough for breads and buns. If you do not have a suitable 1-kg/2-lb loaf dish, use an 18–23-cm/7–9-in deep round dish instead. Alternatively, make 2 450-g/1-lb loaves and bake as in the main recipe but for about 9 minutes. A 15-cm/6-in soufflé dish can be substituted for a small loaf dish.

ALTERNATIVE METHOD
Using 200 C and low microwave setting, cook a 450-g/1-lb loaf for 9–10 minutes or a 1-kg/2-lb loaf for about 15 minutes.

MILK LOAF

 HIGH

Combination:

 MEDIUM

 220 C

MAKES 1 18-cm/ 7-in ROUND LOAF

Illustrated on page 79

450 g/1 lb strong white flour
1 teaspoon salt
50 g/2 oz butter or margarine
2 teaspoons sugar

1 sachet easy-blend dried yeast or
   3 teaspoons ordinary dried yeast
300 ml/$\frac{1}{2}$ pint milk
1 tablespoon sesame seeds

Put the flour in a bowl and stir in the salt. Rub in the butter or margarine. Stir in the sugar and easy-blend yeast. Heat the milk using microwaves only on high for 1 minute, or until lukewarm. If using ordinary dried yeast, sprinkle it over the milk and leave in a warm place until dissolved and frothy.

Make a well in the dry ingredients. Pour in the milk or yeast liquid, then gradually mix in the flour to make a stiff dough. Use your hand to work the dough together. Turn out on to a lightly floured surface and knead thoroughly until very smooth and elastic. Lightly flour the inside of the bowl and put the dough in it. Cover with a dampened cloth or a piece of cling film and leave in a warm place until doubled in size.

Meanwhile, line an 18-cm/7-in round deep dish with greaseproof paper and grease thoroughly. Turn the risen dough out on to a lightly floured surface and knead lightly to knock out the gas. Press the dough into the prepared dish and cover with cling film or a damp cloth. Leave in a warm place until doubled in size and risen above the rim of the dish.

Heat the oven to 220 C. Brush the loaf with a little water and sprinkle with the sesame seeds. Bake the bread at 220 C using medium microwave setting for 10 minutes, or until crisp and very well browned. Leave in the dish for 5 minutes, then turn out on to a wire rack to cool and remove the paper.

SODA BREAD

Combination:

 MEDIUM

 180 C

MAKES 1 SMALL LOAF

Illustrated on page 79

225 g/8 oz plain flour
1 teaspoon bicarbonate of soda

$\frac{1}{2}$ teaspoon salt
150 ml/$\frac{1}{4}$ pint milk

Put the flour in a bowl with the bicarbonate of soda and the salt. Make a well in the middle and pour in the milk. Gradually stir the milk into the flour to make a soft dough. Turn the dough out on to a lightly floured surface and knead very lightly to make a neat round loaf.

Lightly grease a flan dish or similar flat, round dish. Place the loaf on the dish and cut a cross in the top. Bake at 180 C using medium microwave setting for 10 minutes, or until the bread is risen and browned. Transfer to a wire rack to cool – the bread tastes best served warm.

BARA BRITH

 HIGH

Combination:

 MEDIUM

 250 C

MAKES 1 LARGE LOAF

◆ Although it is not traditional, you can always cook this loaf in a round dish – try an 18–23-cm/7–9-in soufflé dish for example.

350 g/12 oz strong white flour
50 g/2 oz butter or margarine
3 tablespoons soft brown sugar
1 sachet easy-blend dried yeast or
   3 teaspoons ordinary dried yeast
1 teaspoon mixed spice

50 g/2 oz currants
50 g/2 oz raisins
50 g/2 oz chopped mixed peel
100 ml/4 fl oz milk
1 egg, beaten

Put the flour in a bowl and rub in the butter or margarine. Stir in the sugar, easy-blend yeast, spice, fruit and peel. Heat the milk using microwaves only on high for 30 seconds. If using ordinary dried yeast, sprinkle it over the milk and leave in a warm place until dissolved and frothy.

Make a well in the dry ingredients and pour in the warmed milk or yeast liquid. Add the egg and mix in the dry ingredients to make a stiff dough. Turn out on to a lightly floured surface and knead thoroughly until smooth and elastic, about 10 minutes. Flour the inside of the mixing bowl and put the dough in it. Cover with a piece of cling film or a damp cloth and leave in a warm place until doubled in size.

Meanwhile, line a 1-kg/2-lb loaf dish with greaseproof paper and grease thoroughly. Turn the risen dough out on to a floured surface and knead lightly to knock out the gas. Press the dough into the prepared dish and cover with cling film or a damp cloth. Leave in a warm place until well risen. Heat the oven to 250 C.

Bake the bara brith at 250 C using medium microwave setting for 10–12 minutes, or until the top of the loaf is well browned and crisp. Leave in the dish for a few minutes, then turn out on to a wire rack to cool and remove the paper.

CHELSEA BUNS

◆ HIGH

Combination:

◆ MEDIUM

◆ 250 C

MAKES 6

225 g/8 oz strong white flour
½ teaspoon salt
½ teaspoon sugar
50 g/2 oz butter or margarine
1 sachet easy-blend dried yeast or
   3 teaspoons ordinary dried yeast

150 ml/¼ pint milk
Filling
100 g/4 oz dried mixed fruit
1 teaspoon mixed spice
50 g/2 oz soft brown sugar
2 tablespoons clear honey or golden syrup

In making the dough, follow the method given in Basic Bread, on page 80.

Line the base of a large flan dish with a circle of greaseproof paper and grease thoroughly. Mix the fruit with the spice and sugar for the filling.

Turn the risen dough out on to a lightly floured surface and knead lightly to knock out all the gas. Roll out the dough into a 25 × 20-cm/10 × 8-in oblong. Spread the filling mixture over the dough, leaving a small gap round the edge. Roll up the dough from the short side. Pinch the edges together firmly to keep the filling in, then cut the roll into eight 2.5-cm/1-in slices. Place these round the edge of the prepared dish. Cover with oiled cling film and leave in a warm place until well risen. The buns should touch each other when risen. Heat the oven to 250 C.

Bake the buns at 250 C using medium microwave setting for 8 minutes or until well risen, firm and browned. Put the honey or syrup in a mug or basin and warm using microwaves only on high for 30 seconds. Leave in the dish for 5 minutes, then carefully lift the ring of buns on to a wire rack to cool. Glaze with the honey or syrup while still hot. These taste best eaten warm.

LIGHT MALT LOAF

Combination:

 MEDIUM

◆ 250 C

MAKES 1 LARGE LOAF

◆ A very light, almost spongy, loaf that can also be cooked in an 18–23-cm/7–9-in soufflé dish.

225 g/8 oz strong white flour
50 g/2 oz butter or margarine
1 sachet easy-blend dried yeast or
   3 teaspoons ordinary dried yeast
50 g/2 oz dark soft brown sugar

50 g/2 oz sultanas
1 teaspoon mixed spice
2 tablespoons malt extract
150 ml/$\frac{1}{4}$ pint milk
2 eggs, beaten

Put the flour in a bowl and rub in the butter or margarine until the mixture resembles fine breadcrumbs. Stir in the easy-blend yeast, sugar, sultanas and spice. Mix the malt extract and milk, then heat using microwaves only on high for 1 minute. Stir well. If using ordinary dried yeast sprinkle it over the warm milk mixture and leave in a warm place until dissolved and frothy.

Make a well in the middle of the dry ingredients. Add the eggs and the milk mixture or yeast liquid. Gradually beat the dry ingredients into the liquid until a smooth, thick batter is formed. Beat hard until the batter has an elastic consistency. Line a 1-kg/2-lb loaf dish with greaseproof paper and grease thoroughly. Pour the batter into the dish and cover with a piece of cling film. Leave in a warm place until the batter has risen to double its size. Heat the oven to 250 C.

Bake the malt loaf at 250 C using medium microwave setting for about 12 minutes, or until firm and browned on top. Leave the bread in the dish for 5 minutes, then turn it out on to a wire rack to cool. Remove the paper when cold. Serve the bread sliced and buttered.

WALNUT TEABREAD

 HIGH

Combination:

 MEDIUM

◆ 220 C

MAKES 1 LARGE LOAF

◆ If you do not have a suitable loaf dish, then use a deep round dish instead, allowing plenty of room for the mixture to rise.

175 g/6 oz mixed dried fruit
300 ml/$\frac{1}{2}$ pint warm tea
225 g/8 oz plain flour
1 teaspoon bicarbonate of soda
2 teaspoons mixed spice

75 g/3 oz margarine
3 tablespoons orange marmalade
100 g/4 oz soft brown sugar
100 g/4 oz walnuts, chopped
2 eggs, beaten

Put the fruit in a bowl and pour in the tea. Leave to soak for 30 minutes. Heat the oven to 220 C. Line a 1-kg/2-lb loaf dish with greaseproof paper, then grease thoroughly.

Sift the flour, bicarbonate of soda and spice into a bowl. Mix the margarine with the marmalade and sugar in a basin, then heat using microwaves only on high for 1 minute, or until the marmalade and margarine melt. Make a well in the middle of the dry ingredients and pour in the melted mixture. Add the walnuts and eggs, then pour in the fruit with the tea.

Gradually beat the dry ingredients into the moist mixture to form a smooth, thick batter. Pour the batter into the prepared dish and bake at 220 C using medium microwave setting for 12 minutes. The teabread should be well risen and deeply cracked down the middle. It should feel soft and springy to the touch. Leave in the dish for 5 minutes, then turn out on to a wire rack to cool and remove the paper. Serve warm or cold, sliced and buttered.

CURRANT BUNS

 HIGH

Combination:

 MEDIUM

 250 C

MAKES 6

Illustrated on page 79

225 g/8 oz strong white flour
½ teaspoon salt
25 g/1 oz butter
1 tablespoon sugar
1 sachet easy-blend dried yeast or
   3 teaspoons ordinary dried yeast

100 g/4 oz currants
150 ml/¼ pint milk
Glaze
2 tablespoons sugar
2 tablespoons milk

Put the flour in a bowl and add the salt. Rub in the butter, then stir in the sugar, easy-blend yeast and currants. Heat the milk using microwaves only on high for about 30 seconds or until lukewarm. If you are using ordinary dried yeast, then sprinkle it over the warm milk and leave it in a warm place until the yeast granules have dissolved and the liquid is frothy. Make a well in the dry ingredients, then pour in the milk or yeast liquid. Gradually mix to make a firm dough, using your hand to gather the dough together. On a lightly floured surface, knead the dough thoroughly until smooth and elastic. Lightly flour the inside of the mixing bowl, put the dough back in it and cover with a dampened cloth or a piece of cling film. Leave in a warm place until doubled in size. Line the base of a 25-cm/10-in quiche dish, or large flat dish, with greaseproof paper. Grease well.

Turn the risen dough out on to a lightly floured surface and knead it very briefly. Cut into six pieces. Shape each piece of dough into a neat bun and place on the prepared dish. Arrange the buns so that they sit round the edge of the dish. As they rise they will touch each other and they will be joined when cooked. Cover with a piece of oiled cling film and leave in a warm place until the buns are well risen.

Bake the buns at 250 C using medium microwave setting for about 8–10 minutes, or until browned. Mix the sugar and milk in a large basin which can go into the hot oven. Cook using microwaves only on high for 1½–2 minutes. Check that the mixture does not boil over. Brush this glaze over the hot buns and transfer them to a wire rack to cool completely. Serve split and buttered, or toasted and buttered.

SWEET SCONE ROUND

Combination:

 MEDIUM

 220 C

MAKES 8 WEDGES

225 g/8 oz self-raising flour
1 teaspoon baking powder
50 g/2 oz margarine
50 g/2 oz raisins

25 g/1 oz sugar
1 egg, beaten
2 tablespoons milk, plus extra to glaze

Put the flour in a bowl and add the baking powder. Rub in the margarine until the mixture resembles fine breadcrumbs. Stir in the raisins and sugar, then make a well in the middle. Add the egg and milk and gradually work in the dry ingredients to make a soft dough. Grease a flan, or similar flat, dish. Turn the scone dough out on to a lightly floured surface. Knead very quickly and lightly until smooth, then roll out or flatten into a 20-cm/8-in circle and place on the dish. Mark into eight wedges and brush with a little milk. Bake at 220 C using medium microwave setting for 8–10 minutes, or until risen and browned. Transfer to a wire rack to cool, then serve warm with butter.

SAVOURY SCONE

Combination:

 MEDIUM

◆ 250 C

MAKES 8 WEDGES

225 g/8 oz self-raising flour
50 g/2 oz margarine
1 small onion, finely chopped
2 teaspoons dry mustard

75 g/3 oz Cheddar cheese, grated
salt and pepper
150 ml/¼ pint milk
1 egg, beaten, to glaze

Put the flour in a bowl. Add the margarine and rub it into the mixture resembles fine breadcrumbs. Stir in the onion, mustard, cheese and a little seasoning. Pour in the milk and stir to make a soft dough. Turn the dough out on to a lightly floured surface and knead very lightly to make a smooth ball. Press or roll into a 20-cm/8-in circle.

Lightly grease a flan or other flat dish and put the scone circle on it. Mark into eight wedges. Brush with a little beaten egg and bake at 250 C using medium microwave setting for 10–12 minutes. Transfer to a wire rack to cool. Serve warm, with butter, a wedge of Cheddar cheese and some pickled onions.

SCONE PIZZA

 HIGH

Combination:

 MEDIUM

◆ 250 C

SERVES 4

◆ Using this scone base, you can add any of your favourite pizza toppings – fish, meat, or vegetables. For some tasty combinations, refer to Topping Ideas for Pizza on pages 64–5.

Topping
1 large onion or 2 small onions, chopped
2 tablespoons oil (olive oil, if you like the flavour)
2–3 cloves garlic, crushed
1 teaspoon dried marjoram
2 tablespoons tomato purée
salt and freshly ground black pepper
150 g/5 oz mozzarella cheese, sliced

1 (50-g/2-oz) can anchovies
8–10 black olives, stoned and halved
Base
225 g/8 oz self-raising flour
3 teaspoons baking powder
salt
50 g/2 oz butter or margarine
1 egg, beaten
75 ml/3 fl oz milk

First prepare the topping. Put the onion in a basin with the oil and garlic. Cook using microwaves only, on high for 3 minutes. Stir in the marjoram and tomato purée and add seasoning to taste. Heat the oven to 250 C.

For the base, put the flour in a bowl and add the baking powder. Sprinkle in a pinch of salt, then rub in the butter or margarine, until the mixture resembles fine breadcrumbs. Mix in the egg and milk to make a soft scone dough. Grease a 25-cm/10-in quiche dish. On a lightly floured surface, lightly knead the dough until just smooth, then press it out, or roll it out, into a 23-cm/9-in circle. Lift the circle on to the prepared dish.

Spread the onion, garlic and tomato purée mixture over the dough. Arrange the mozzarella on top. Drain the anchovies, reserving oil, and chop them, then sprinkle them evenly over the mozzarella. Top with the olives and sprinkle with the reserved oil.

Bake the pizza at 250 C using medium microwave setting for 8–10 minutes, or until risen and browned round the edges. Serve freshly cooked.

Top Mocha Cake *(page 93)*
Bottom Fruit and Nut Cake *(page 92) and*
Cherry and Almond Cake *slices (page 89)*

CAKES AND
· BISCUITS ·

VICTORIA SANDWICH

Combination:

 MEDIUM

◆ 200 C

MAKES 1 18-cm/
7-in CAKE

175 g/6 oz butter or margarine
175 g/6 oz sugar
½ teaspoon vanilla essence
3 eggs

175 g/6 oz self-raising flour
225 g/8 oz jam
caster sugar to dust

Grease two 18-cm/7-in round shallow dishes (cake, soufflé, or fairly deep flan dishes). Line each with a circle of greaseproof paper and grease the paper. Heat the oven to 200 C.

Beat the butter or margarine with the sugar and vanilla essence until very pale and soft. Gradually beat in the eggs, adding a little of the flour if the mixture begins to curdle. Use a metal spoon to fold in the remaining flour as lightly as possible.

Turn the mixture into the prepared dishes, dividing it equally between them. Smooth the surface of each and bake at 200 C and medium microwave setting. Put one cake dish straight on the turntable, and the second cake on the rack above. If your oven has a wide shelf, then put both cakes on the same level.

Cook for 8–9 minutes, then remove the top cake from the oven and move the cake below up on to the rack to finish cooking. Cook for a further 3–4 minutes. The cooked cakes should be lightly browned and firm to the touch. Turn both cakes out on to a wire rack to cool and remove the lining paper.

Sandwich the cakes together with jam and sprinkle the top with a little caster sugar.

VARIATIONS

Chocolate Cake Substitute 25 g/1 oz cocoa powder for an equal quantity of the flour. Sandwich the cakes together with whipped cream or chocolate butter icing. To make a chocolate butter icing, beat 50 g/2 oz butter with 75 g/3 oz sifted icing sugar until smooth and soft. Dissolve 1 tablespoon cocoa powder in 2 tablespoons boiling water, cool slightly and beat into the icing. Top the cake with melted chocolate and sprinkle with a little icing sugar.

Lemon Cake Add the grated rind of 1 lemon to the creamed mixture instead of the vanilla essence. Sandwich the cooled cakes together with lemon curd and top the cake with a lemon glacé icing. To make the icing, sift 100 g/4 oz icing sugar into a bowl and beat in 1–2 tablespoons lemon juice.

ALTERNATIVE METHOD

Cook using 200 C and low microwave setting for 10 minutes. Remove top cake, move bottom cake up and cook for a further 1–2 minutes.

CHERRY AND ALMOND CAKE

Combination:

 MEDIUM

◆ 220 C

MAKES 1 18-cm/
7-in CAKE

Illustrated on page 87

225 g/8 oz glacé cherries
175 g/6 oz butter or margarine
175 g/6 oz sugar
3 eggs

$\frac{1}{4}$ teaspoon almond essence
200 g/7 oz self-raising flour
100 g/4 oz blanched almonds, chopped
2 tablespoons milk

Heat the oven to 220 C. Line an 18-cm/7-in deep, round dish with greaseproof paper and grease the paper thoroughly. Halve the cherries, put them in a sieve and wash them under warm water. Drain the fruit and dry it on absorbent kitchen paper. Set aside.

Beat the butter or margarine and sugar together until very pale and creamy. Beat in the eggs and almond essence, adding a little of the flour if the mixture begins to curdle. Add a little flour to the cherries and toss them in it to coat them completely. Fold the remaining flour into the cake mixture using a metal spoon. Fold in the cherries, then fold in the almonds and milk.

Turn the mixture into the prepared dish and lightly smooth the top. Bake at 220 C using medium microwave setting for 13–15 minutes, or until the cake has risen and lightly browned. Leave the cake in the dish for a few minutes, then turn it out on to a wire rack to cool. Remove the paper when the cake has cooled completely.

MADEIRA CAKE

Combination:

 HIGH

◆ 220 C

MAKES 1 18-cm/
7-in CAKE

175 g/6 oz butter
175 g/6 oz sugar
grated rind of 1 lemon
3 eggs

200 g/7 oz self-raising flour
2 tablespoons milk
strip of candied citron peel

Heat the oven to 220 C. Line an 18-cm/7-in deep round dish with greaseproof paper and grease the paper thoroughly. The paper should stand about 2.5 cm/1 in above the rim of the dish.

Beat the butter, sugar and lemon rind together until pale and very creamy. Beat in the eggs, adding a spoonful of the flour if the mixture begins to curdle. Use a metal spoon to fold the flour into the mixture as lightly as possible. Lastly fold in the milk. Turn the mixture into the prepared dish, spreading it lightly and evenly. Lay the strip of candied peel on top of the cake.

Bake the cake at 220 C using medium microwave setting for 13–15 minutes, or until the cake is well risen and lightly browned. Leave the cake in the dish for a few minutes, then turn it out on to a wire rack. Remove the paper when the cake has cooled.

ALTERNATIVE METHOD
Cook at 220 C using low microwave setting for 17 minutes.

CHOCOLATE ALMOND CAKE

Combination:

 MEDIUM

 200 C

MAKES 1 18-cm/
7-in CAKE

◆ For an elaborate
decoration use 300 ml/½
pint double cream and
pipe a border of cream
swirls round the top of the
cake before adding the
chocolate and nut
topping. Allow the melted
chocolate to cool slightly
before pouring it over the
middle of the cake.

175 g/6 oz butter or margarine
175 g/6 oz sugar
¼ teaspoon almond essence
3 eggs
175 g/6 oz self-raising flour
25 g/1 oz cocoa powder
1 teaspoon baking powder

100 g/4 oz ground almonds
2 tablespoons milk
150 ml/¼ pint double cream
2 teaspoons icing sugar
100 g/4 oz plain chocolate
25 g/1 oz butter
50 g/2 oz blanched almonds, chopped

Line and grease an 18-cm/7-in deep, round dish. Beat the butter or margarine and
sugar with the almond essence until very pale and creamy. Beat in the eggs, adding
a little of the flour if the mixture begins to curdle. Sift the flour with the cocoa and
baking powders. Fold these dry ingredients into the creamed mixture using a metal
spoon. Fold in the ground almonds and the milk.

Turn the mixture into the prepared dish and smooth the top. Bake at 200 C using
medium microwave setting for 12–15 minutes, or until the cake is well risen and
firm on top. Leave the cake in the dish for a few minutes, then transfer it to a wire
rack to cool. Remove the paper when the cake has cooled completely.

When the cake is cold, slice it horizontally in half. Whip the cream and icing
sugar until the mixture stands in soft peaks. Sandwich the cake with the filling. Put
the chocolate and butter in a small basin and melt using microwaves only on
medium setting for 1–2 minutes. Stir well, then swirl the chocolate over the top of
the cake and sprinkle with almonds. Leave the topping to set before serving.

CARROT CAKE

Combination:

 MEDIUM

 200 C

MAKES 1 18-cm/
7-in CAKE

◆ Colour marzipan and shape it into carrots to make an unusual decoration for this scrumptious cake.

100 g/4 oz butter or margarine
100 g/4 oz sugar
grated rind and juice of 1 orange
2 eggs
175 g/6 oz self-raising flour

1 teaspoon baking powder
1 teaspoon cinnamon
225 g/8 oz carrots, grated
50 g/2 oz walnuts, chopped

Line an 18-cm/7-in deep, round dish with greaseproof paper. The paper should stand about 2.5 cm/1 in above the rim of the dish. Grease the paper thoroughly. Heat the oven to 200 C.

Beat the butter or margarine with the sugar and orange rind until very pale and soft. Gradually beat in the eggs, adding a little of the flour if the mixture begins to curdle.

Sift the remaining flour with the baking powder and cinnamon. Use a metal spoon to fold the flour mixture, carrot and walnuts into the creamed ingredients. Lastly fold in the orange juice. Turn the mixture into the prepared dish and lightly smooth the top. Bake at 200 C using medium microwave setting for 13—15 minutes, or until the cake is well risen, lightly browned and set. Leave in the dish for 5 minutes, then turn the cake out on to a wire rack to cool completely and remove the paper.

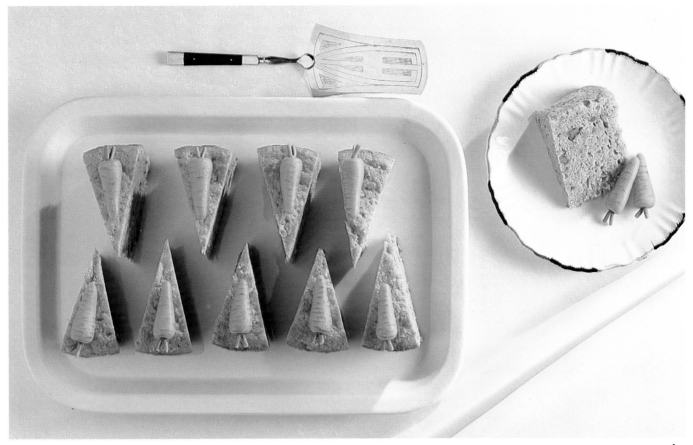

FRUIT AND NUT CAKE

Combination:

 MEDIUM

 180 C

MAKES 1 18-cm/
7-in CAKE

Illustrated on page 87

175 g/6 oz butter or margarine
175 g/6 oz sugar
grated rind and juice of 1 orange
3 eggs

200 g/7 oz self-raising flour
350 g/12 oz mixed dried fruit
100 g/4 oz walnut pieces, roughly chopped

Heat the oven to 180 C. Line an 18-cm/7-in deep round dish with greaseproof paper and grease the paper thoroughly. The paper should stand about 2.5 cm/1 in above the rim of the dish.

Beat the butter or margarine, sugar and orange rind together until very pale and creamy. Beat in the eggs, adding a little of the flour if the mixture begins to curdle. Sprinkle a spoonful of the flour over the dried fruit and mix well. Add the rest of the flour to the creamed mixture and fold it in very lightly using a metal spoon. Sprinkle in the fruit and nuts, then fold these ingredients in using the metal spoon. Lastly fold in the orange juice.

Turn the mixture into the prepared dish and lightly smooth the top. Bake at 180 C using medium microwave setting for 20–22 minutes, or until the cake has risen and lightly browned on top. Leave the cake in the dish for a few minutes, then turn it out on to a wire rack to cool. Remove the paper when the cake has cooled completely.

FRUIT CAKE

Combination:

 MEDIUM

 180 C

MAKES 1 18-cm/
7-in CAKE

◆ To achieve a dark, rich result fruit cake should be cooked by traditional, very slow methods. This recipe is a speedy alternative – the resulting cake is quite full-flavoured but it cannot be directly compared with a dark, long-baked cake.

100 g/4 oz butter
100 g/4 oz dark soft brown sugar
1 tablespoon black treacle
grated rind and juice of 1 orange
grated rind of 1 lemon
4–6 tablespoons brandy or rum
100 g/4 oz raisins
100 g/4 oz currants
100 g/4 oz sultanas

50 g/2 oz chopped mixed peel
50 g/2 oz blanched almonds, chopped
50 g/2 oz glacé cherries
3 eggs, lightly beaten
175 g/6 oz plain flour
50 g/2 oz ground almonds
$\frac{1}{2}$ teaspoon ground mixed spice
$\frac{1}{2}$ teaspoon ground cinnamon
$\frac{1}{4}$ teaspoon grated nutmeg

Line and grease an 18-cm/7-in cake dish. Beat the butter, sugar and treacle together until very soft and creamy. Beat in the fruit rinds. Put the orange juice in a large basin. Add 2 tablespoons of the brandy or rum, then mix in the raisins, currants, sultanas, peel and nuts. Wash the cherries, quarter them and add to the fruit. Mix well.

Gradually beat the eggs into the creamed mixture, adding enough flour to prevent the mixture from curdling. Add the remaining flour and the ground almonds, then sprinkle in the spices. Mix thoroughly. Lastly add all the fruit and the juices. Mix thoroughly then turn into the dish. Smooth the top and bake at 180 C using medium microwave setting for 20–25 minutes. A skewer inserted into the middle of the cake should come out clean.

Cover the cake with a tea-towel and leave in the dish for 1 hour. Cool on a wire rack. Pierce the base of the cake with a fork. Slowly drizzle the remaining brandy over the cake. Leave for 10 minutes, then wrap in greaseproof paper and place in an airtight tin. Mature for a month before eating.

MOCHA CAKE

Combination:

 MEDIUM

 200 C

**MAKES 1 18-cm/
7-in CAKE**

Illustrated on page 87

175 g/6 oz butter or margarine
175 g/6 oz sugar
3 eggs
175 g/6 oz self-raising flour
2 tablespoons instant coffee
2 tablespoons boiling water
Filling and Icing
75 g/3 oz butter

175 g/6 oz icing sugar, sifted
2 tablespoons cocoa powder
1 tablespoon boiling water
2 tablespoons rum or brandy
Decoration
175 g/6 oz walnut halves

Base-line and grease two 18-cm/7-in round sandwich cake dishes. Heat the oven to 200 C.

Beat the butter or margarine with the sugar until very pale and soft. Beat in the eggs, adding a little of the flour if the mixture begins to curdle. Dissolve the coffee in the boiling water and leave to cool slightly. Use a metal spoon to fold the flour into the creamed mixture. Lastly fold in the coffee.

Turn the mixture into the prepared dishes, dividing it equally between them. Smooth the top and bake the cakes, one on the turntable and the second on the wire rack, at 200 C using medium microwave setting, for 7–7½ minutes, or until the top cake is risen and golden. It should feel firm and springy to the touch. Remove the top cake from the oven and transfer the cake from the turntable to the rack. Cook for a further 2½–3 minutes, or until lightly browned and cooked.

Leave the cakes in the dishes for a few minutes, then turn them out on to a wire rack to cool. Remove the greaseproof paper.

To make the filling and icing, beat the butter with the icing sugar until pale and very soft. Mix the cocoa powder with the boiling water, then gradually stir in the rum or brandy. Beat this flavouring into the butter icing. Reserve a few of the walnut halves and chop the remainder.

Sandwich the cakes together with a little of the butter icing. Spread a little round the sides of the cake. Put the chopped walnuts on a sheet of greaseproof paper and roll the sides of the cake in them. Spread a thin layer of butter icing over the top of the cake. Put the remaining butter icing in a piping bag fitted with a star nozzle and pipe a border round the top edge of the cake. Decorate with the reserved walnut halves.

ORANGE GINGERBREAD

 HIGH

Combination:

 MEDIUM

◆ 220 C

MAKES 1 LARGE LOAF

◆ If you don't have a big loaf dish, then use a large round dish instead, making sure it leaves plenty of room for the mixture to rise.

75 g/3 oz margarine
75 g/3 oz soft brown sugar
100 g/4 oz golden syrup
2 tablespoons black treacle
175 g/6 oz plain flour
1 tablespoon ground ginger

1 teaspoon cinnamon
1 teaspoon bicarbonate of soda
grated rind of 2 oranges and juice of
 1 orange
150 ml/¼ pint milk
1 egg, beaten

Heat the oven to 220 C. Line a 1-kg/2-lb loaf dish with greaseproof paper and grease thoroughly.

Place the margarine, sugar, syrup and treacle in a basin and heat using microwaves only on high for 1½–2 minutes, or until melted. Stir well.

Sift the flour, ginger, cinnamon and soda into a bowl and make a well in the middle. Add the orange rind and juice, the melted mixture and the milk. Beat the egg into the liquid ingredients, then gradually beat in the dry ingredients to make a smooth, thick batter. Turn the batter into the prepared dish and bake at 220 C using medium microwave setting for 10 minutes, or until the gingerbread is risen and set. When cooked it will be deeply cracked down the middle.

Leave the gingerbread in the dish to cool for 10 minutes, then turn it out on to a wire rack to cool completely. Remove the paper when the gingerbread has cooled completely. Wrap closely in foil or cling film and keep for at least 24 hours before eating.

SHORTBREAD

Combination:

 MEDIUM

 190 C

MAKES 8 PIECES

175 g/6 oz butter
75 g/3 oz caster sugar, plus extra to dust

150 g/5 oz plain flour
100 g/4 oz self-raising flour

Beat the butter with the caster sugar until very pale and soft. Gradually beat in the flours to make a firm dough.

Lightly grease a 23–25-cm/9–10-in flan dish. Turn the dough out on to a lightly floured surface and knead it briefly, until smooth. Press or roll it out into a circle measuring about 20–23 cm/8–9 in across. Place the shortbread in the dish and prick it all over with a fork. Mark the edge with the prongs of the fork and mark eight wedges with the point of a knife.

Bake at 190 C using medium microwave setting for about 8–10 minutes, or until the shortbread is lightly browned. Leave in the dish for a few minutes, then carefully separate the wedges and put them on a wire rack to cool completely. Dust with a little caster sugar while still hot.

ALTERNATIVE METHOD
The shortbread can be baked at 190 C using low microwave setting for 11–12 minutes.

Savarin (page 105)

· PUDDINGS ·

APPLE DUMPLINGS

Combination:

 MEDIUM

 250 C

SERVES 4

350 g/12 oz plain flour
175 g/6 oz margarine or 75 g/3 oz margarine
   and 75 g/3 oz lard
about 3–4 tablespoons water
4 medium cooking apples, peeled and cored
4 tablespoons raisins

2 tablespoons soft brown sugar
grated rind of 1 orange
½ teaspoon ground cinnamon
milk to glaze
caster sugar to dust

Put the flour in a bowl and rub in the fat until the mixture resembles fine breadcrumbs. Gradually mix in the water to make a short pastry dough. Mix the pastry together with your fingertips, then cut it into four. Heat the oven to 250 C.

Take a portion of pastry and roll it out into a circle large enough to enclose an apple. Place an apple in the middle. Mix the raisins with the sugar, orange rind and cinnamon. Press a quarter of this mixture into the middle of the apple. Brush the edges of the pastry with a little water, then fold the pastry around the apple to enclose it completely. Press the pastry together well to seal in the filling, at the same time trimming off any thick pastry joins. Turn the dumpling over so that the joins are underneath. If you like, roll out any trimmings to make pastry leaves, brush these with a little water, then place them on top of the dumpling. Make the other dumplings in the same way.

Place the dumplings on a flan dish and brush with a little milk. Sprinkle with a little sugar and bake at 250 C using medium microwave setting for 8 minutes, or until the pastry is cooked and golden.

Serve the dumplings freshly cooked with whipped cream or custard.

EVE'S PUDDING

Combination:

 MEDIUM

 200 C

SERVES 4

675 g/1½ lb cooking apples, peeled, cored and
   sliced
25 g/1 oz sugar
Topping
75 g/3 oz butter, softened, or soft margarine
75 g/3 oz sugar

1 egg
75 g/3 oz self-raising flour
1 teaspoon baking powder
2 tablespoons milk
caster sugar to sprinkle (optional)

Heat the oven to 200 C. Put the apple slices in a dish, sprinkling them with the sugar as they are layered up.

For the topping, put all the ingredients in a bowl and beat vigorously until thoroughly combined and pale. This is best done using an electric food mixer but since the quantities are small the mixture can be beaten by hand.

Spread the topping over the apples, then bake at 200 C using medium microwave setting for 15 minutes, or until the sponge topping is risen and lightly browned. Sprinkle over a little caster sugar, if liked. Serve freshly cooked, with cream or custard.

APPLE FLAN

Combination:

 MEDIUM

 250 C

SERVES 6–8

◆ Firm, ripe pears also make a good filling for this flan.

Pastry
175 g/6 oz plain flour
75 g/4 oz butter or margarine
25 g/1 oz sugar
1 egg yolk
Filling
675 g/1½ lb cooking apples, peeled, cored and thickly sliced

2–4 tablespoons sugar
25 g/1 oz butter
Apricot Glaze
100 g/4 oz apricot jam
1–2 tablespoons water

Put the flour in a bowl and rub in the butter or margarine until the mixture resembles coarse breadcrumbs. Mix in the sugar and egg yolk to make a soft dough. Press together with the fingertips and wrap in polythene. Chill for 10 minutes before rolling. Roll out the pastry on a lightly floured surface into a circle large enough to line a 23-cm/9-in flan dish. Trim the excess pastry by rolling the rolling pin over the edge of the dish. Prick the base all over, then chill for 15 minutes.

Place a piece of greaseproof paper in the pastry case and put a handful of baking beans or dried peas in it. Bake at 250 C medium microwave setting for 5 minutes. Fill the half-baked pastry case with the apple slices, arranging them neatly in two layers and sprinkling a little sugar over. The amount of sugar you add depends on how sour the fruit is. Remember that the glaze is very sweet, so do not overdo the sugar. Dot with the butter.

Bake the flan at 250 C using medium microwave setting for 12–15 minutes. For the glaze, mix the apricot jam with 1 tablespoon of the water in a basin and heat in the microwave only on high for 30 seconds. Press through a sieve and thin down further if necessary. Heat for another 30 seconds, then brush over the apples. Serve the flan hot, warm or cold, with whipped cream.

HAWAII CRUMBLE

Combination:

 MEDIUM

 220 C

SERVES 4–6

◆ This tastes great – do try it. You will be surprised.

450 g/1 lb cooking apples, peeled, cored and sliced
1 (432-g/15¼-oz) can pineapple chunks in natural juice
2 pieces preserved stem ginger, chopped
50 g/2 oz sugar

Topping
75 g/3 oz plain flour
40 g/1½ oz butter
50 g/2 oz sugar
50 g/2 oz desiccated coconut

Put the apple slices in a dish with the pineapple and ginger. Mix together with the sugar and press down well. Heat the oven to 220 C.

For the topping, put the flour into a bowl and rub in the butter until the mixture resembles fine breadcumbs. Stir in the sugar and coconut. Sprinkle this topping over the fruit and bake the crumble at 220 C using medium microwave setting for about 10 minutes, or until browned on top. Serve hot with cream or ice cream.

ALTERNATIVE METHOD
The crumble can be cooked at 220 C using low microwave setting for 15 minutes.

ALMOND UPSIDE-DOWN PUDDING

Combination:

 MEDIUM

 200 C

SERVES 6–8

◆ If when you turn this pudding out it is slightly under-cooked on top, simply cook using microwaves only for about 30 seconds.

1 (420-g/14.8-oz) can peach halves, drained
6–8 glacé cherries
175 g/6 oz butter, softened, or soft margarine
175 g/6 oz sugar
½ teaspoon almond essence

3 eggs
175 g/6 oz self-raising flour
1 teaspoon baking powder
75 g/3 oz ground almonds
2 tablespoons milk

Heat the oven to 200 C. Base-line and grease a 23-cm/9-in soufflé dish or other straight-sided round dish. (If you do not have a straight-sided dish, use a casserole dish instead.)

Arrange the peach halves in the dish: put a glacé cherry in each of the stone cavities, then turn the peaches cut side down. Put all the remaining ingredients in a bowl and beat vigorously until very soft and creamy, and pale in colour. Spoon this mixture into the dish over the peaches. Spread evenly, then bake at 200 C, using medium microwave setting, for 13–15 minutes, or until the pudding is set and browned on top.

Turn the pudding out on to a serving platter and remove the lining paper. Serve hot with custard or cream.

ALTERNATIVE METHOD
Cook at 200 C using high microwave setting for 3 minutes, then reduce the microwave setting to low and cook for a further 15–20 minutes.

CLAFOUTIS

Combination:

 MEDIUM

 250 C

SERVES 4–6

50 g/2 oz butter
1 (454-g/16-oz) can stoned cherries, drained
100 g/4 oz plain flour
50 g/2 oz sugar

2 eggs
300 ml/½ pint milk
caster sugar to dust

Use about half the butter to thoroughly grease an 18-cm/7-in round dish. Put the cherries in the dish. Heat the oven to 250 C.

Put the flour in a bowl and stir in the sugar. Make a well in the middle. Break in the eggs and add the milk; beat the latter two ingredients together, then gradually start incorporating the flour to make a smooth batter. Beat thoroughly to make sure that there are no lumps. Pour the batter over the cherries and dot with the remaining butter.

Bake the clafoutis at 250 C using medium microwave setting for 15 minutes, or until risen, set and golden. Dust with a little caster sugar and serve immediately, with single or soured cream.

APPLE AND BANANA OATY

 HIGH

Combination:

 MEDIUM

 220 C

SERVES 4

3 tablespoons golden syrup
50 g/2 oz butter or margarine
grated rind and juice of 1 orange
50 g/2 oz walnuts, chopped
175 g/6 oz rolled oats

450 g/1 lb cooking apples, peeled, cored and sliced
2 large bananas, sliced
25 g/1 oz sugar

Mix the syrup, butter or margarine, orange rind and juice in a basin and heat using microwaves only on high for 1 minute. Heat the oven to 220 C.

Mix the walnuts and oats into the syrup. Layer the apple and banana slices in a large dish, sprinkling with the sugar. Top with the oat mixture and bake at 220 C using medium microwave setting for 8 minutes, or until the topping is browned and cooked. Serve freshly cooked with cream or custard, or vanilla ice cream.

BREAD AND BUTTER PUDDING

Combination:

 MEDIUM

 220 C

SERVES 4

75 g/3 oz butter
6 slices bread, crusts removed
100 g/4 oz raisins
50 g/2 oz demerara sugar

grated rind of 1 large orange
$\frac{1}{2}$ teaspoon ground cinnamon
2 eggs
300 ml/$\frac{1}{2}$ pint milk

Butter the bread and cut the slices into strips. Layer the bread in a dish with the raisins. Sprinkle each layer with a little sugar, orange rind and cinnamon. Beat the eggs with the milk, then pour this mixture over the layers of bread. Leave to soak for at least 15 minutes. The pudding can be covered and left to soak overnight.

Bake at 220 C using medium microwave setting for 15 minutes, or until golden brown and set. Serve freshly baked, with an orange flavoured custard sauce.

TOPPING IDEA FOR BREAD AND BUTTER PUDDING
Make a simple orange custard to complement the pudding: mix 2 tablespoons cornflour with grated rind of 1 orange, 2 tablespoons sugar, 2 egg yolks and a little milk taken from 450 ml/$\frac{3}{4}$ pint. Heat the remaining milk using microwaves only on high for 4 minutes. Pour the hot milk on to the cornflour mixture, whisking all the time. Cook on high for a further 2 minutes or until thickened. Whisk thoroughly before serving with the pudding.

LEMON CUSTARD TART

Combination:

◈ MEDIUM

◆ 180 C

SERVES 6–8

Pastry
175 g/6 oz plain flour
100 g/4 oz butter or margarine
25 g/1 oz sugar
2 tablespoons water
Filling
4 tablespoons lemon curd

grated rind of 1 lemon
25 g/1 oz sugar
2 large eggs
450 ml/¾ pint milk

Heat the oven to 180 C. Put the flour in a bowl and rub in the butter or margarine until the mixture resembles coarse breadcrumbs. Stir in the sugar and mix in the water to make a soft pastry dough. Chill for 5 minutes.

Roll out the pastry on a lightly floured surface into a circle large enough to line a 23-cm/9-in flan dish. Trim off the excess pastry by rolling the rolling pin round the rim of the dish. Prick the base and chill for 15 minutes. Place a piece of greaseproof paper in the pastry case and sprinkle a handful of baking beans or dried peas over it. Bake at 180 C using medium microwave setting for 7 minutes.

Remove the paper and beans and allow the pastry to cool slightly, then spread the lemon curd over the base. Beat the lemon rind, sugar and eggs together, then gradually beat in the milk. Strain the mixture through a fine sieve into the flan. Bake at 180 C using medium microwave setting for 15 minutes, or until the custard has set and lightly browned on top. Serve warm or cold, with single cream if you like.

LEMON SAUCE PUDDING

Combination:

◈ MEDIUM

◆ 220 C

SERVES 4–6

100 g/4 oz butter or margarine
100 g/4 oz sugar
grated rind and juice of 2 lemons

2 eggs, separated
75 g/3 oz self-raising flour
250 ml/8 fl oz milk

Grease a 23-cm/9-in dish (or any suitable dish which looks attractive enough to serve the pudding in). Heat the oven to 220 C.

Beat the butter or margarine with the sugar and lemon rind until very pale and soft. Beat in the egg yolks and the lemon juice. Stir in the flour, then gradually stir in the milk. Whisk the egg whites until they stand in stiff peaks. Use a metal spoon to fold the whites into the pudding.

Turn the mixture into the dish and bake at 220 C using medium microwave setting for 8–10 minutes. The sponge topping should be risen, lightly browned and set. Underneath there will be a thick, rich, lemon sauce which tastes delicious. Serve freshly baked.

QUEEN OF PUDDINGS

Combination:

 MEDIUM

 180 C/250 C

SERVES 6

100 g/4 oz fresh white breadcrumbs
4 eggs
175 g/6 oz sugar
grated rind of 1 lemon

a little grated nutmeg
600 ml/1 pint milk
6–8 tablespoons jam

Heat the oven to 180 C. Grease a 23-cm/9-in dish. Place the breadcrumbs in the dish. Separate 2 of the eggs; put the yolks in a bowl and set the whites aside. Add the whole eggs to the yolks. Beat in 50 g/2 oz of the sugar, the lemon rind and nutmeg. Gradually pour in the milk, then pour the mixture into the dish over the breadcrumbs. Press down with a fork and set aside for 15 minutes.

Bake at 180 C using medium microwave setting for 6–8 minutes, or until almost set. Remove from the oven and allow to stand for 5 minutes. Heat the oven to 250 C. Spread the jam over the pudding. Whisk the egg whites until they stand in stiff peaks, then use a metal spoon to fold in the remaining sugar. Spread the meringue over the pudding, forking it into peaks. Bake at 250 C using medium microwave setting for about 3 minutes to lightly brown the meringue. If the meringue is not browned after 3 minutes, then continue cooking using just convection setting – do not use microwaves any longer or the meringue will overcook before browning. Serve freshly cooked.

RASPBERRY MILLE FEUILLE

 HIGH

Combination:

 MEDIUM

◆ **250 C**

SERVES 6

1 (250-g/8¾-oz) packet puff pastry,
    defrosted if frozen
icing sugar to dust
4 tablespoons raspberry jam

1–2 tablespoons sweet sherry
350 g/12 oz raspberries, hulled
150 ml/¼ pint double cream, whipped

Heat the oven to 250 C. Cut three double oblongs of greaseproof paper, 15 × 25 cm/6 × 10 in but no smaller. Roll out the pastry into an oblong measuring slightly larger than 23 × 38 cm/9 × 15 in. Trim and cut into three 23 × 13-cm/9 × 5-in pieces. Place each piece of pastry on a piece of greaseproof paper and prick all over. Chill for 10 minutes. The reason for putting the pastry on the paper is that there are few ovens which will accommodate a large oblong dish.

Bake the pastry, two pieces in one batch, placing one paper straight on the turntable and the second on the wire rack above. Cook at 250 C using medium microwave setting for 3 minutes. Remove the top piece of pastry which should be puffed and lightly browned. Place on a wire rack. Transfer the pastry from the turntable to the rack and put the third piece on the turntable. Cook for a further 1–1½ minutes by which time the second piece of pastry should be cooked. Transfer the last piece of pastry to the rack and cook for a final 1½–2 minutes. Dust the top of the best piece of pastry quite thickly with icing sugar while still hot. Cool.

Warm the raspberry jam using microwaves only on high for 30–60 seconds. Stir in the sherry and mix in the raspberries. Sandwich the pastry together with the raspberry mixture and cream, placing the piece dusted with icing sugar on top.

ORANGE AND WALNUT BAKEWELL PUDDING

Combination:

MEDIUM

◆ 200 C

SERVES 4–6

◆ Good old Bakewell pudding given a face-lift! Here is a fine example of how to make the best of your combination microwave oven.

1 quantity Shortcrust Pastry (page 68)
Filling
4–6 tablespoons jam
100 g/4 oz butter or margarine
100 g/4 oz sugar

grated rind and juice of 1 orange
2 eggs
100 g/4 oz self-raising flour
100 g/4 oz walnuts, roughly chopped

Roll out the pastry on a lightly floured surface into a round large enough to line a 25-cm/10-in flan dish. Trim the edges off the pastry by rolling the rolling pin round the rim of the dish. Prick the base all over.

Spread the jam over the pastry. Heat the oven to 200 C. For the filling, beat the butter or margarine with the sugar and orange rind until very soft and pale. Beat in the eggs, adding a little of the flour if the mixture begins to curdle. Use a metal spoon to fold in the remaining flour and the orange juice.

Spread the filling over the jam and sprinkle the walnuts on top. Bake at 200 C using medium microwave setting for about 15 minutes, or until the filling is risen, golden and set. Serve hot with a custard sauce or leave to cool and serve cut into wedges.

TREACLE TART

HIGH

Combination:

MEDIUM

250 C

SERVES 6–8

9 tablespoons golden syrup
25 g/1 oz butter
grated rind and juice of 1 lemon
1 quantity Shortcrust Pastry (page 68)

$\frac{1}{2}$ teaspoon mixed spice
$\frac{1}{2}$ teaspoon cinnamon
75 g/3 oz fresh breadcrumbs

First prepare the filling. Mix the syrup, butter, lemon rind and juice in a large basin and heat using microwaves only on high for 1 minute, or until the butter has melted. Stir well and set aside.

Heat the oven to 250 C. Roll out the pastry on a lightly floured surface into a circle large enough to line a 23-cm/9-in tart plate. (If you do not have a tart plate, then use a shallow flan dish.) Chill for 10 minutes. Prick the base all over, then bake at 250 C using medium microwave setting for 5 minutes.

Stir the spices and breadcrumbs into the syrup mixture. Spread the mixture over the pastry and bake at 250 C using medium microwave setting for 4–5 minutes. Serve warm or cold, with cream if you like.

SAVARIN

 HIGH

Combination:

 MEDIUM

 250 C

SERVES 4–6

Illustrated on page 95

◆ This dessert is one of those outstanding specialities which is in fact not too difficult to prepare. With your combination cooker you'll find that it is also not too time-consuming to cook. You can vary the fruit salad to suit your tastes, purse and seasonal availability. The important thing is to keep it colourful and fresh.

225 g/8 oz strong white flour
1 sachet easy-blend dried yeast or 3
  teaspoons ordinary dried yeast
2 tablespoons sugar
6 tablespoons milk
4 eggs
100 g/4 oz butter

50 g/2 oz sugar
150 ml/¼ pint water
4 tablespoons rum
Fruit Salad
225 g/8 oz strawberries, hulled
1 kiwi fruit, peeled and sliced
50 g/2 oz seedless grapes

Put the flour into a bowl with the easy-blend yeast and sugar. Warm the milk using microwaves only on high for 30 seconds. If you are using ordinary dried yeast, sprinkle it over the milk and leave in a warm place until dissolved and frothy.

Beat the eggs into the milk or yeast liquid. Melt the butter using microwaves only on high for about 2 minutes. Make a well in the middle of the flour. Pour in the egg mixture and the butter. Gradually beat in the flour to make a thick batter. Beat hard until the batter becomes quite elastic. Thoroughly grease a 23-cm/9-in ring dish with a 1.15-litre/2-pint capacity. Pour the batter into it and leave in a warm place until the batter rises to the top of the dish. Meanwhile, heat the oven to 250 C. Bake the savarin at 250 C using medium microwave power for 8 minutes. Leave in the dish while the syrup is prepared.

Mix the sugar and water in a large basin. Heat using microwaves only on high for 3–5 minutes, or until the syrup has boiled and reduced slightly. Make sure that it does not boil over the top of the basin. Stir the rum into the syrup.

Turn the savarin out on to a wire rack. Put a plate or dish under the rack to catch any syrup which drips down. Prick the savarin with a fork and carefully spoon the syrup over it so that it soaks in. Leave to cool. Mix the ingredients for the fruit salad and add any leftover syrup. Serve the cooled savarin filled with the fruit salad. Offer lightly whipped double cream with it to make a stunning dessert.

RICH CHOCOLATE PUDDING

Combination:

 MEDIUM

 200 C

SERVES 6

◆ The melted chocolate drops and nuts give a pleasantly sticky topping.

100 g/4 oz butter or margarine
100 g/4 oz golden syrup
2 eggs
100 g/4 oz self-raising flour
25 g/1 oz cocoa powder

3 tablespoons rum or brandy
50 g/2 oz chocolate cooking drops
25 g/1 oz nibbed almonds or walnuts,
  chopped

Heat the oven to 200 C. Thoroughly grease a 15-cm/6-in dish. Beat the butter or margarine with the syrup until very soft and pale. Beat in the eggs. Sift the flour with the cocoa powder, then fold the mixture into the creamed ingredients using a metal spoon. Lastly fold in the rum or brandy.

Turn the mixture into the dish and smooth the top. Mix the chocolate drops with the nuts and sprinkle over the pudding. Bake at 200 C using medium microwave setting for 7–10 minutes, or until the pudding has risen and set. Serve hot, straight from the dish, with cream, custard or brandy sauce.

BAKED CHEESECAKE

SERVES 8

Base
50 g/2 oz self-raising flour
50 g/2 oz ground almonds
40 g/1½ oz butter
2 tablespoons sugar
1 egg yolk
Topping
75 g/3 oz sugar

225 g/8 oz cream cheese
grated rind and juice of 2 large lemons
50 g/2 oz sultanas
75 g/3 oz self-raising flour
3 eggs
icing sugar to dust

First prepare the dish. Cut a long, wide strip of greaseproof paper and fold it over three times in a lengthwise direction. Place this strip in an 18-cm/7-in dish so that it lies across the base, up the sides and over the edge. This will be used to lift the cooked cheesecake out of the dish. Cut a circle of greaseproof paper and lay it on the bottom of the dish, over the strip. Grease the paper and sides of the dish. Heat the oven to 180 C.

Put the flour and almonds in a bowl, then rub in the butter and stir in the sugar Bind with the egg yolk and press this sweet dough into the base of the dish. Prick all over and chill for 10 minutes. Bake at 180 C using medium microwave setting for 2 minutes.

For the topping, beat the sugar with the cream cheese, and lemon rind. Gradually beat in the lemon juice, sultanas and flour. Lastly beat in the eggs. Pour into the dish over the base and bake at 180 C using medium microwave setting for about 25 minutes, or until well risen and browned on top. Leave to cool in the dish – the cheesecake will sink back as it cools.

Run a knife round the inside of the dish to loosen the cheesecake, then carefully lift it out with the help of the strip of greaseproof paper. Dust generously with icing sugar and serve.

Plaice with Shrimp Sauce (page 111)

MICROWAVES
· ONLY ·

◆ SOUNDS AND STARTERS

CHICKEN STOCK

MAKES 900 ml/1½ PINTS

1 large chicken joint	1 onion chopped
bay leaf	1 stick celery, sliced
sprig of thyme	900 ml/1½ pints boiling water
2 parsley sprigs	salt and pepper
2 carrots, sliced	

Put the chicken joint in a large casserole dish. Add the herbs and vegetables. Pour in 300 ml/½ pint of the water and cover. Cook on high for 10 minutes. Pour in the remaining boiling water and leave to stand for 15 minutes.

Strain, setting aside the chicken and squeezing all the juice out of the vegetables. Discard the chicken skin, dice all the meat and add to the stock. (Alternatively reserve the chicken for another use.) Add seasoning to taste. Use as required, as a base for soups, sauces and casseroles.

CREAM OF CHICKEN SOUP

SERVES 4

900 ml/1½ pints chicken stock (preceding recipe)	1 large potato, diced
	salt and white pepper
1 onion, chopped	150 ml/¼ pint single cream
25 g/1 oz butter	4 tablespoons chopped parsley
2 tablespoons plain flour	

Make the chicken stock according to the instructions, adding the chopped chicken meat.

Put the onion in a large casserole dish or mixing bowl. Add the butter and cook on high for 3 minutes. Stir in the flour, add the potato and stir in 300 ml/½ pint of the stock. Cover and cook on high for 15 minutes.

Blend in a liquidiser until smooth, return to the bowl and add the remaining stock. Cook, uncovered, on high for 10 minutes, taste and adjust the seasoning. Stir in the cream, heat for 2 minutes without boiling and add the parsley. Serve piping hot.

BEEF STOCK

MAKES 900 ml/1½ PINTS

This is really a cheat's beef stock. The best beef stock calls for marrow bones and lengthy simmering but this is a good alternative and may be used in stews, soups and sauces.

100 g/4 oz lean bacon, chopped	bay leaf
	large parsley sprig
225 g/8 oz good minced beef	sprig of thyme
1 large onion, chopped	900 ml/1½ pints boiling water
2 large carrots, chopped	salt and pepper

Put the bacon, beef and vegetables in a casserole dish with the herbs. Pour in 600 ml/1 pint of the boiling water and cover. Cook on high for 10 minutes, stir well, cook for a further 5 minutes. Pour in the remaining boiling water and leave to stand for 15 minutes.

Strain the stock, pressing all the goodness out of the ingredients. Taste and adjust the seasoning as necessary.

BEEF AND TOMATO SOUP

SERVES 4

900 ml/1½ pints beef stock (preceding recipe)	2 sticks celery, sliced
	1 kg/2 lb tomatoes, roughly chopped
1 large onion, chopped	
2 cloves garlic, crushed	salt and freshly ground black pepper
25 g/1 oz butter	
1 large potato, diced	4 tablespoons chopped parsley

Make the stock according to the instructions. Put the onion, garlic and butter in a large casserole dish or mixing bowl and cover. Cook on high for 3 minutes. Pour in 300 ml/½ pint of the stock, then add the vegetables and cover.

Cook on high for 10 minutes, stir well, cook for a further 10 minutes. Blend in a liquidiser until smooth, then sieve to remove the tomato seeds. Stir in the rest of the stock and season to taste. Cook, uncovered, for 5–8 minutes, stir in the parsley and serve.

SPICY LENTIL SOUP

SERVES 4

1 large onion, chopped
2 carrots, chopped
2 sticks celery, chopped
knob of butter
1 clove garlic, crushed
100 g/4 oz red lentils
2 tablespoons ground coriander
900 ml/1½ pints chicken stock
    (see page 108) or vegetable
    stock if preferred

4 tablespoons chopped parsley
    or 2 tablespoons chopped
    coriander leaves
salt and freshly ground black
    pepper
croûtons (see below)

Put the onion, carrot, celery and butter in a large casserole dish or bowl. Add the garlic and cover, then cook on high for 5 minutes.

Stir in the lentils and spice and pour in 600 ml/1 pint of the stock. Stir, cover and cook on high for 20 minutes. Stir in the remaining stock, the parsley or coriander and seasoning to taste. Cook, uncovered, for 5–8 minutes, then serve piping hot.

CROÛTONS

Cut sliced bread into tiny cubes, discarding the crusts if you like. Place the cubes on a piece of absorbent kitchen paper on a plate. Cover with a second piece of paper and microwave on high. For 4 slices of bread allow about 4–6 minutes, until the bread is really dry and crisp.

Melt some butter in a small basin, adding chopped herbs and/or garlic, if you like. Allow about 30–60 seconds on full power for the butter. Toss the croûtons in the butter, leave for a minute or two, then drain very briefly on absorbent kitchen paper to remove excess fat. Use as required.

The dry croûtons can be stored for ages in an airtight jar and you can toss them in melted butter just before use. For reduced calories you can always use the crunchy croûtons dry.

CHICKEN LIVER PÂTÉ

SERVES 4

450 g/1 lb chicken livers,
    roughly chopped
2 cloves garlic, crushed
1 small onion, finely chopped
100 g/4 oz butter
salt and freshly ground black
    pepper

2 tablespoons brandy
1 tablespoon chopped parsley
1 teaspoon chopped fresh
    thyme
thyme sprigs to garnish

Put the chicken liver in a basin or casserole dish with the garlic and onion. Add a knob of the butter and cover. Cook on high for 5 minutes, stir well, re-cover and cook for 3–5 minutes, until cooked. Stir most of the remaining butter into the liver, reserving a little for topping the individual pâtés.

Blend the liver in a liquidiser until smooth. Add seasoning to taste, the brandy and herbs. Put into four ramekin dishes. Melt the remaining butter for 1 minute, then spoon over the pâtés to form a thin covering. Place a thyme sprig on each and chill. Serve with crisp toast.

GARLIC MUSHROOMS

SERVES 4

450 g/1 lb small button
    mushrooms, wiped
50 g/2 oz butter or 50 ml/2 fl oz
    olive oil
3 cloves garlic, crushed
salt and freshly ground black
    pepper

4 tablespoons chopped parsley
    or 2 tablespoons chopped
    basil
Parmesan cheese, grated, to
    serve (optional)

Put the mushrooms in a large casserole dish or bowl with the butter or oil, and garlic. Stir well, then cover and cook on high for 5–7 minutes. Stir in seasoning to taste and the parsley or basil. Serve immediately, topped with Parmesan cheese if you like. Crusty bread is the ideal accompaniment.

GARLIC HERB BREAD

SERVES 4

50 g/2 oz butter
2 cloves garlic, crushed
4 tablespoons chopped fresh
    herbs, including parsley,
    thyme, marjoram, tarragon,
    a little mint, a little rosemary
    and some basil

1 short French loaf or Granary
    stick

Beat the butter with the garlic and herbs. Cut the loaf into slices, then butter the slices and press back together into two portions. Put on a plate and heat on high for about 1 minute. Serve at once.

MOULES MARINIÈRE

SERVES 2–4

1 kg/2 lb mussels	150 ml/¼ pint water
handful of oatmeal	salt and freshly ground black
1 small onion, finely chopped	pepper
1 stick celery, chopped	**Thickening**
1 clove garlic, crushed	large knob of butter
(optional)	2 tablespoons plain flour
25 g/1 oz butter	2 tablespoons chopped parsley
bay leaf	to garnish
150 ml/¼ pint dry white wine	

Put the mussels in a bucket of cold water with the oatmeal and leave overnight (this process removes any impurities and grit which the mussels may have ingested). Drain and wash the shellfish, then thoroughly scrub the shells. Pull away the black hairy 'beards' which protrude from the shells. Tap any open shells and discard any that do not close immediately.

Place the onion, celery and garlic (if used) in a large bowl or casserole dish with the butter. Cover and cook using microwaves only on high for 3 minutes. Add the bay leaf, wine and water. Sprinkle in seasoning to taste and re-cover, then continue to cook on high for a further 5 minutes or until the liquid is boiling.

Add the mussels and cover the dish. Cook on high for 5 minutes or until all the shells have opened. For the thickening, beat the butter and flour together until smooth. Lift the mussels from the cooking dish using a large slotted spoon. Put them into warmed individual bowls (four if you are serving a starter, two for a main course), discarding any that have not opened. Whisk the butter and flour mixture into the cooking juices and cook in the microwave on high for 3 minutes, or until slightly thickened.

Ladle the sauce over the mussels and sprinkle with chopped parsley. Serve immediately, with warmed, crusty bread.

POACHED SALMON STEAKS

SERVES 4

4 (175-g/6-oz) salmon steaks	4 sprigs of dill
50 g/2 oz butter	salt and freshly ground white
2 tablespoons dry white wine	pepper

Arrange the salmon steaks in a flan dish, placing them as far apart as possible. Top each with a little butter and sprinkle with the wine. Place a sprig of dill on each steak, then cover the dish with microwave cling film or an upturned plate.

Cook on high for 7–8 minutes, then leave to stand for 2–3 minutes. Season lightly before serving, with the cooking juices poured over. Alternatively, leave to cool then serve with home-made mayonnaise.

Moules Marinière

SIMPLE FISH CASSEROLE

SERVES 4

Use this recipe as a guide for preparing basic fish dishes in sauce. You can add chopped green or red pepper, sweetcorn, cut French beans, peas or carrots. Serve with rice, pasta or mashed potatoes. If you like, top with cheese and breadcrumbs and grill.

675 g/1½ lb white fish fillet,	225 g/8 oz button mushrooms,
skinned and cut into chunks	sliced
(try cod, haddock or coley)	salt and freshly ground white
1 onion, finely chopped	pepper
25 g/1 oz butter	2 tablespoons chopped parsley
2 tablespoons plain flour	150 ml/¼ pint single cream
300 ml/½ pint fish stock or milk	

Remove any bones from the fish. Put the onion and butter in a casserole dish and cover. Cook on high for 3 minutes. Stir in the flour, add the fish stock or milk and whisk well. Add the sliced mushrooms and cook on high for 5 minutes.

Whisk the sauce well, then add the fish and seasoning to taste. Cover and cook on high for 5 minutes, then stir well. Cook for a further 3–5 minutes, or until the fish is cooked. Stir in the parsley and cream, cook for 1 minute to heat. Serve at once.

SOLE VÉRONIQUE

SERVES 4

If you like, substitute less expensive white fish for the sole in this recipe, for example try plaice or whiting. The fillets can be cut into portions instead of being rolled if you like. Add watercress for extra colour.

8 sole fillets, skinned
salt and freshly ground white pepper
25 g/1 oz butter
2 tablespoons plain flour

300 ml/½ pint dry white wine
2 tablespoons chopped parsley (optional)
100 g/4 oz seedless white grapes

Lay the fish fillets flat on a board, skinned side up and sprinkle with the seasoning. Roll up from the head end and arrange in a casserole dish.

In a small basin, melt the butter on high for 1 minute. Stir in the flour, then whisk in the wine and cook on high for 2 minutes. Whisk well, then stir in the parsley. Pour this sauce over the fish. Scrape all the sauce out of the basin. Cover the casserole and cook the sole on high for 5 minutes. Turn the fish, add most of the grapes to the casserole, reserving just a few for garnish. Re-cover and continue to cook on high for a final 5 minutes. Leave to stand for 2–3 minutes, then serve garnished with the reserved grapes.

Sole Véronique

CREAMED TUNA

SERVES 4

1 large onion, finely chopped
1 (198-g/7-oz) can tuna in oil
3 tablespoons plain flour
salt and freshly ground black pepper

300 ml/½ pint milk
100 g/4 oz mushrooms, thinly sliced
2 tablespoons chopped parsley
50 g/2 oz cheese, grated

Put the onion in a large basin or casserole dish. Add the oil from the tuna and cook on high for 3 minutes. Stir in the flour, seasoning and the milk, pouring it in slowly to prevent lumps forming. Whisk well. Cook on high for 4 minutes.

Whisk the sauce, then add the flaked fish, sliced mushrooms, parsley and cheese. Cook for a further 5 minutes, or until the sauce has thickened. Stir well and serve on cooked rice or pasta.

PLAICE WITH SHRIMP SAUCE

SERVES 4

Illustrated on page 107

8 plaice fillets, skinned
25 g/1 oz butter
2 tablespoons dry white wine
2 tablespoons plain flour
250 ml/8 fl oz milk
2 teaspoons tomato purée

salt and freshly ground black pepper
1 (200-g/7-oz) can shrimps, drained
4 spring onions, trimmed and finely chopped

Roll up the plaice fillets from the head end, with the skinned side inside. Arrange in a casserole dish and dot with the butter. Sprinkle in the wine, cover the dish and cook on high for 3–5 minutes. Rearrange the fish, turning the rolls over, then re-cover and cook for a further 3–5 minutes, or until just cooked.

Use a draining spoon to transfer the fish rolls to a serving platter and keep hot. Whisk the flour into the cooking juices, then whisk in the milk and tomato purée. Add seasoning to taste and the shrimps. Cook on high for 5–7 minutes, or until the sauce boils and thickens. Stir well, add the spring onion and pour over the plaice. Serve at once.

◆ SNACKS

SCRAMBLED EGGS

For each portion:
2 eggs
1 tablespoon milk

knob of butter
salt and pepper

Beat the eggs with the milk in a basin. Add a knob of butter and a little seasoning. Cook using microwaves only on high. Whisk the eggs frequently during cooking to obtain a creamy result. As a guide, watch the eggs as they cook, then remove them from the oven and whisk well as the edge of the mixture begins to set and rise. The eggs should be whisked three or four times during cooking. Follow the cooking times given below.

2 eggs ——————— $2-2\frac{1}{2}$ minutes
4 eggs ——————— $3\frac{1}{2}-4$ minutes
6 eggs ——————— $6-6\frac{1}{2}$ minutes

SPICY PRAWNS

SERVES 4

This is a dish of curried prawns to be served with cooked rice — Basmati rice will give the best flavour. Alternatively offer Indian breads or pitta bread to scoop up the prawn curry. It really is delicious and an excellent light supper dish.

1 large onion, finely chopped
2 cloves garlic, crushed
2 tablespoons oil
2 teaspoons ground ginger
1 tablespoon ground coriander
2 teaspoons ground cumin
bay leaf
$\frac{1}{4}-\frac{1}{2}$ teaspoon chilli powder

1 (425-g/15-oz) can chopped tomatoes
450 g/1 lb frozen peeled cooked prawns
salt and freshly ground black pepper
2 tablespoons chopped coriander leaves (optional)

Put the onion, garlic and oil in a large casserole dish. Cover and cook on high for 3 minutes. Stir in all the remaining ingredients apart from the coriander leaves. Cover and cook on high for 5 minutes. Stir well, then cook for a further 5 minutes. Stir well, sprinkle with the coriander leaves, if used, and serve at once.

CHICKEN LIVER SAVOURY

SERVES 4

Serve this tasty chicken-liver mixture on hot toast, or with cooked rice or pasta for a more substantial snack. The large quantity of parsley is an important ingredient — so try not to skimp on it.

1 onion, finely chopped
1 clove garlic, crushed
25 g/1 oz butter
2 tablespoons plain flour
450 g/1 lb chicken livers, roughly chopped

100 g/4 oz button mushrooms, sliced
150 ml/$\frac{1}{4}$ pint soured cream
salt and freshly ground black pepper
4 tablespoons chopped parsley

Put the onion, garlic and butter in a basin or casserole dish and cook on high for 3 minutes. Stir in the flour and chicken liver. Cover the dish and cook on high for 3 minutes. Add the mushroom, stir well and re-cover the dish. Continue cooking on high for another 4–5 minutes, or until the liver is cooked to your liking. Stir in the cream and add seasoning to taste. Heat for 2 minutes, then add the parsley and serve.

SPICY CHICK PEA SNACK

SERVES 4

Serve this tasty mixture of chick peas, spices and yogurt with pitta bread or Indian breads if you live near a shop which sells them. Corners of the bread are used to scoop up the chick pea mixture.

1 large onion, finely chopped
2 cloves garlic, crushed
2 tablespoons oil
1 teaspoon ground ginger
$\frac{1}{2}$ teaspoon curry powder
2 teaspoons ground coriander
1 teaspoon ground cumin
2 (375-g/13.2-oz) cans chick peas, drained

salt and freshly ground black pepper
1 tablespoon chopped mint or $\frac{1}{2}$ teaspoon concentrated mint sauce
2 tablespoons thick natural yogurt

Put the onion in a basin with the garlic and oil. Cook on high for 3 minutes, then stir in all the remaining ingredients and cook on high for 3–5 minutes, or until the chick peas are very hot. Serve at once.

HOT MUSHROOM DIP

SERVES 4

100 g/4 oz small, white button
  mushrooms, chopped
a little lemon juice
1 small onion, finely chopped
1 clove garlic, crushed
25 g/1 oz butter
1 tablespoon plain flour
50 g/2 oz cheese, grated (a mild
  hard cheese is best –
  Caerphilly or Lancashire for
  example)

2 tablespoons mayonnaise
150 ml/¼ pint soured cream
salt and freshly ground black
  pepper
1 tablespoon chopped parsley

Mix the chopped mushrooms with the lemon juice. Put the onion in a basin with the garlic and butter and cook on high for 3 minutes. Stir in the flour, cheese and mayonnaise. Cook on high for 3 minutes, then stir in the soured cream, mushroom and seasoning to taste. Cook on high for 3 minutes, then add the parsley and serve with crackers, breadsticks or any suitable savoury snacks.

HOT BACON SANDWICHES

For each sandwich:

2 thick slices fresh bread or hot
  toast
a little butter

a little prepared mustard or
  other relish of your choice
2 rashers rindless bacon

Have the bread or toast ready for when the bacon is cooked. Spread it with a little butter and mustard or any other relish.

Place the bacon rashers on a large plate or on a special microwave roasting rack and cover with a double thick piece of absorbent kitchen paper. Cook on high for the following times:

2 rashers	1½–2 minutes
4 rashers	2½ minutes
6 rashers	4½ minutes
8 rashers	5–6 minutes

Drain the cooked bacon if necessary, then sandwich it between the bread or toast and serve at once.

ADDITIONAL FILLINGS

Add any of the following to complement the bacon:
Sliced tomatoes.
Sliced onion, separated into rings.
Open mushrooms cooked with a knob of butter for 1–4 minutes to just cook them. The time will depend on the quantity. Use high power setting and aim to just melt the butter on the mushrooms. Sandwich with the bacon.

PITTA SNACK

SERVES 4

4 pieces pitta bread
4 slices cooked ham
4 slices cheese (Cheddar,
  Lancashire or any hard
  cheese)

2 large tomatoes, sliced

Split the pitta down one side, separating the bread to make pockets. Slide a slice of ham into each piece, folding the meat over to fit it in. Slide in a slice of cheese and a few slices of tomato.

Heat the pitta, two pieces at a time, on a large plate. Cook on high for 2–3 minutes, or until the cheese has melted. Cut in half to serve.

ALTERNATIVE FILLINGS
Garlic sausage instead of ham.
Frankfurters with tomato slices and onion rings.
Peanut butter with ham and cheese.
Cheese and onion.
Sliced smoked sausage with onion rings and tomato slices.
Cooked chicken, sliced, with cream cheese (just a little) and thinly sliced mushrooms.
Flaked tuna fish with a little cream cheese and chopped onion.
Mashed sardines with lemon juice, onion rings and tomato slices.

WELSH RAREBIT

SERVES 4

50 ml/2 fl oz beer
1 tablespoon prepared mustard
225 g/8 oz cheese, grated

salt and freshly ground black
  pepper
fresh buttered toast to serve

Pour the beer into a basin and stir in the mustard. Cook on high for 2 minutes, then gradually beat in the cheese and seasoning to taste. Continue to cook on high for 3 minutes, or until the cheese has just melted. Beat well and serve spread on hot toast. Put under a hot grill to brown if you like.

Alternatively, the mixture can be kept covered in the refrigerator for several days and spread on toast to be browned under the grill.

◆ VEGETABLES

CAULIFLOWER CHEESE

SERVES 4

1 large cauliflower
600 ml/1 pint cheese sauce
  (see page 120)

2 tablespoons fresh
  breadcrumbs
a little grated cheese

Trim the outer leaves from the cauliflower and discard any thick stalk. Wash and shake dry the cauliflower head, leaving it slightly damp. Put in a large casserole dish or bowl and cover. Cook on high for about 15 minutes, or until tender.

Make the cheese sauce. Drain any liquid from the cauliflower then pour the sauce over and sprinkle with the breadcrumbs and cheese. Brown under a hot grill. Serve at once.

◆ The cauliflower can be partly cooked in advance for 10 minutes and the sauce poured over, then sprinkled with the breadcrumbs and cheese and cooled. Chill until required. To heat, cook at 250 C using medium microwave setting for 10–15 minutes, or until the cauliflower cheese is bubbling hot and browned.

RED CABBAGE WITH APPLE

SERVES 4

This well-known dish tastes good with pork – grilled chops for example – or lamb. It is an excellent accompaniment for grilled continental sausages.

1 large onion, chopped
25 g/1 oz butter
2 tablespoons oil
450 g/1 lb red cabbage,
  shredded
350 g/12 oz cooking apples,
  peeled, cored and sliced

2 tablespoons sugar
1 tablespoon cider vinegar
salt and freshly ground black
  pepper

Put the onion, butter and oil in a large casserole dish and cook on high for 3 minutes. Add the cabbage and cover the dish. Cook on high for 5 minutes.

Stir well, add the apple slices, sugar and cider vinegar, then cook for a further 5 minutes. Taste and add the seasoning before serving.

Vegetable Curry

VEGETABLE CURRY

SERVES 4

1 large aubergine, trimmed and
  cut into chunks
salt and freshly ground black
  pepper
1 large onion, chopped
2 cloves garlic, crushed
4 tablespoons oil
1 large potato, cubed
1 large carrot, diced
1 large parsnip, diced

2 sticks celery, sliced
2 tablespoons ground coriander
2 teaspoons ground fenugreek
1 tablespoon ground cumin
$\frac{1}{4}$–$\frac{1}{2}$ teaspoon chilli powder
4 whole cardamoms
bay leaf
150 ml/$\frac{1}{4}$ pint boiling water
225 g/8 oz cauliflower florets

Place the aubergine in a colander and sprinkle with salt, then leave in the sink or over a bowl for 3 minutes. Rinse and dry well.

Place the onion in a large casserole dish with the garlic and oil. Cover and cook on high for 3 minutes. Add the potato, carrot, parsnip and celery. Re-cover and cook on high for 5 minutes. Stir in the aubergine, spices and bay leaf and re-cover. Cook for a further 5 minutes on high.

Stir in the water and cauliflower. Cover the casserole and cook on high for a further 10–15 minutes, or until all the vegetables are tender and the flavour well developed. Taste and season as required. Serve with pilau rice at once.

COURGETTES WITH ALMONDS

SERVES 4

450 g/1 lb courgettes, sliced
50 g/2 oz butter
4 spring onions, chopped

25 g/1 oz flaked almonds
salt and freshly ground black
   pepper

Put the courgette slices in a large casserole dish with half the butter. Cover and cook on high for 4 minutes. Add the spring onion, stir well, then cook for a further 3–4 minutes.

Put the almonds in a mug with the remaining butter and cook on high for 3–4 minutes, or until the almonds are browned. Pour over the courgette mixture, add seasoning to taste and stir. Serve at once.

VARIATION

Instead of the spring onions you can add 100 g/4 oz sliced mushrooms to the courgettes. Omit the flaked almonds but sprinkle with almonds if you like.

CELERIAC WITH CREAM CHEESE

SERVES 4

1 (1-kg/2-lb) celeriac, peeled
   and cut into chunks
4 tablespoons water
salt and freshly ground black
   pepper

50 g/2 oz cream cheese
4 tablespoons soured cream

Put the celeriac in a large casserole dish with the water. Cover and cook on high for 12–15 minutes, or until the vegetable is tender. Rearrange the pieces once during cooking. Drain.

Mash the celeriac, then beat in the remaining ingredients. Heat on high for 2 minutes, stir well and serve.

CREAMED LEEKS

SERVES 4

300 ml/½ pint Béchamel Sauce
   (page 120)
450 g/1 lb leeks, sliced
25 g/1 oz butter

50 g/2 oz cream cheese
   flavoured with garlic and
   herbs (for example, Boursin)
salt and freshly ground black
   pepper

Prepare the sauce. Make sure the leeks are thoroughly washed. Shake off the excess water and put the sliced leeks in a large casserole dish. Add the butter, cover the dish and cook on high for 5 minutes. Stir well, cook for a further 5 minutes.

Stir the sauce and cheese into the leek, adding seasoning to taste. Cook for a further 2 minutes and serve.

CREAMED SPINACH

SERVES 4

This basic recipe for spinach can be used to create a variety of interesting dishes. For example, use the spinach to fill a lasagne, or pancakes, or in a creamy cannelloni dish.

450 g/1 lb fresh spinach,
   trimmed, washed and
   shredded
25 g/1 oz butter
2 tablespoons plain flour

150 ml/¼ pint single cream
salt and freshly ground black
   pepper

Put the damp spinach in a large roasting bag and secure the opening loosely with an elastic band. Cook on high for 5–7 minutes, or until the spinach is cooked. Set aside.

Put the butter in a basin and melt on high for 30 seconds. Stir in the flour and cook on high for a further 30 seconds. Whisk in the cream and cook on high for 2 minutes.

Drain the spinach and add to the cream mixture. Stir well, season to taste and cook on high for 2 minutes. Stir well, then cook for a further 3–4 minutes. Serve at once or use as required.

Glazed Carrots (page 117)

RATATOUILLE

SERVES 4

1 large aubergine, trimmed and
    cut into chunks
salt and freshly ground black
    pepper
50 ml/2 fl oz olive oil
1 red pepper, deseeded and
    chopped

1 large onion, chopped
2 cloves garlic, crushed
225 g/8 oz courgettes, sliced
450 g/1 lb tomatoes, peeled
    and roughly chopped
plenty of chopped parsley

Place the aubergine in a colander and sprinkle with salt. Leave in the sink or over a draining board for 20–30 minutes, then rinse and dry. Place in a large casserole with the oil and mix in the red pepper, onion and garlic.

    Cover and cook on high for 5 minutes, stir well, then cook for a further 5 minutes. Stir in the courgette and tomato, add some of the parsley and re-cover. Cook for 5–8 minutes, or until all the vegetables are cooked. Add seasoning to taste and extra parsley. Serve at once.

SPROUTS WITH CHESTNUTS

SERVES 4

225 g/8 oz chestnuts
450 g/1 lb sprouts

50 g/2 oz butter
salt and freshly ground black
    pepper

Make a good, long split down the side of each chestnut, then thoroughly wash all the nuts and place them, still very wet, in a basin. Cover and cook on high for about 5 minutes, or until tender.

    Wash and trim the sprouts, making a cross in the base of any large ones. Place in a casserole dish, cover and cook on high for 8–10 minutes, or until cooked to taste. Add the butter and the chestnuts, toss well and cook for another 1 minute. Season to taste before serving.

VEGETABLE COOKING CHART

VEGETABLE	COOKING TIME IN MINUTES ON HIGH	COOKING INSTRUCTIONS
Artichokes, globe –4 –2 –1	 20–25 15–17 8–10	Wash and trim off stalk. Snip off leaf tips. Shake off excess water and put in roasting bag. Secure opening loosely with elastic band. Turn halfway through cooking. Leave to stand for 5 minutes, remove centre leaves and hairy choke from middle. Serve hot or cold.
Artichokes, Jerusalem 450 g/1 lb	10–12	Peel and place in dish with 3 tablespoons water and a little lemon juice. Cover and rearrange halfway through cooking. Leave to stand for 2 minutes, then serve with butter and snipped chives.
Asparagus 450 g/1 lb	5–7	Trim off woody stalk ends and wash. Put in roasting bag, secure end loosely with elastic band and rearrange halfway through cooking. Snip off corner of bag and drain over sink or bowl. Stand 3–4 minutes before serving.
Beans, broad 450 g/1 lb shelled weight	7–9	Put in dish with 2 tablespoons water. Cover and stir halfway through cooking. Stand 3 minutes before serving.
Beans, French or runner 450 g/1 lb	6–8	Put beans in dish with 2 tablespoons water. Cover and rearrange halfway through cooking. Stand for 3 minutes before serving.
Beetroot 450 g/1 lb	8–10	Wash and trim; do not peel. Put in dish with 2 tablespoons water. Cover and rearrange halfway through cooking.
Broccoli 450 g/1 lb	7–8	Put in dish with 2 tablespoons water. Cover and rearrange halfway through cooking. Stand 3 minutes before serving.

VEGETABLE	COOKING TIME IN MINUTES ON HIGH	COOKING INSTRUCTIONS
Brussels sprouts 450 g/1 lb	8–10	Put in dish with 2 tablespoons water. Rearrange halfway through cooking.
Cabbage —Savoy type 450 g/1 lb	8–10	Shred, put in dish with 3 tablespoons water. Cover and rearrange halfway through cooking.
—white	10–15	As above; timing depends on required cooked texture.
Carrots 225 g/8 oz (Illustrated on page 115)	5–6	Trim and cut into matchstick strips. Rinse, drain and put in dish with knob of butter, $\frac{1}{2}$ teaspoon sugar and 1 tablespoon water. Rearrange halfway through cooking. Sprinkle with chopped parsley and serve.
Cauliflower —whole (about 450 g/1 lb)	12–15	Trim, wash and shake off water. Place in dish and cover. Stand for 3 minutes before serving.
—florets (about 225 g/8 oz)	5–6	Wash and place in dish or roasting bag. Secure end loosely with elastic band or cover and rearrange halfway through cooking.
Celeriac (1 kg/2 lb)	15–17	Peel, trim and cut into cubes. Wash and put in dish with 4 tablespoons water. Rearrange halfway through cooking.
Corn-on-the-cob —2 cobs —4 cobs	7–8 15–16	Trim cobs, removing all husk. Put in roasting bag with 2 tablespoons water. Stand 2 minutes before serving.
Courgettes	3–5	Trim and slice. Place in dish with knob of butter. Cover and rearrange halfway through cooking.
Leeks	5–7	Trim and slice. Wash well, shake off excess water but leave wet. Place in dish and cover. Stir halfway through cooking.
Marrow 450 g/1 lb	8–10	Peel and cut into cubes. Put in dish with 2 tablespoons water. Cover and rearrange halfway through cooking. Stand 3 minutes before serving.

VEGETABLE	COOKING TIME IN MINUTES ON HIGH	COOKING INSTRUCTIONS
Mushrooms, button (whole) 225 g/8 oz	2–3	Put in dish with generous knob of butter and cover. Stir halfway through cooking and serve sprinkled with chopped parsley.
Onions, 4 large whole	10–12	Place in dish with 2 tablespoons water and cover. Turn over halfway through cooking. Leave to stand for 5 minutes before draining and serving.
Parsnips 675 g/1½ lb	15–17	Peel and cut into chunks. Put in dish with 4 tablespoons water. Stand 3 minutes before draining and mashing with butter and seasoning.
Peas 450 g/1 lb shelled weight	7–10	Wash and place in dish with 2 tablespoons water. Cover and stir halfway through cooking. Serve drained, dotted with butter.
Potatoes —new 450 g/1 lb	5	Scrub and wash, then put in dish with 2 tablespoons water. Stand 3 minutes before serving.
—new 1 kg/2 lb	10–12	As above.
—old, cubed, 1 kg/2 lb	15–18	Peel and cube. Put in dish with 4 tablespoons water. Mash before serving.
baked 1 —2 —3 —4	8 12–15 20–22 25–28	Scrub well, cut out eyes. Prick skin and put on double-thick layer of absorbent kitchen paper. Turn and rearrange halfway through cooking.
Spinach 450 g/1 lb 1 kg/2 lb	5–6 10–12	Wash and shred (if liked). Shake off excess water and put in dish. Cover and stir halfway through cooking.
Spring Greens 450 g/1 lb	7–10	Trim and shred. Place in dish with 3 tablespoons water. Stand 3 minutes. Drain, serve with butter.
Swede 675 g/1½ lb	15–17	Peel and cut into cubes. Put in dish with 3 tablespoons water. Stand 3 minutes before draining. Mash with butter and pepper.

◆ RICE DISHES

COOKED RICE

SERVES 4

225 g/8 oz long-grain white rice	pinch of salt
600 ml/1 pint water	knob of butter

Put the rice in a large basin or bowl, or into a casserole dish. Allow room for the rice to boil up as it cooks. Pour in the water and add the salt. Cover and cook using microwaves only on high for 15 minutes. Leave to stand, covered, for 5 minutes, then add the butter and fork up the grains before serving.

Brown Rice For brown rice allow 750 ml/1¼ pints water and cook for 20–25 minutes instead of 15 minutes. Leave to stand for 2–3 minutes before serving.

PILAU RICE

SERVES 4

2 onions, sliced	4 cardamoms
2 tablespoons oil	225 g/8 oz Basmati rice
1 cinnamon stick	600 ml/1 pint boiling water
bay leaf	25 g/1 oz butter
4 cloves	2 teaspoons black cumin seeds

Put one of the sliced onions in a casserole dish with the oil and cook on high for 3 minutes. Add the cinnamon stick, bay leaf, cloves, cardamoms and rice. Pour in the water, cover the dish and cook on high for 15 minutes. Remove from the oven and set aside.

Put the butter, remaining onion and the cumin seeds in a basin. Cook on high for 5 minutes. Fork up the cooked rice, spoon the onion and cumin mixture over the top serve at once.

PAELLA

SERVES 4

1 green or red pepper, deseeded and chopped	225 g/8 oz long-grain rice
1 onion, chopped	salt and freshly ground black pepper
2 large cloves garlic, crushed	225 g/8 oz frozen peeled cooked prawns
2 tablespoons olive oil	
175-g/6-oz uncooked boneless chicken breast, skinned and cut into small cubes	100 g/4 oz frozen cooked mussels
½ teaspoon saffron strands	100 g/4 oz frozen peas
600 ml/1 pint boiling water	225 g/8 oz tomatoes, peeled and chopped

Put the pepper, onion and garlic in a large casserole dish with the oil and chicken. Cover and cook using microwaves only on high for 8 minutes.

Meanwhile, pound the saffron strands in a pestle and mortar,

Paella

then add a little of the boiling water. Add the rice to the chicken mixture and stir well. Pour in the saffron liquid and the remaining boiling water. Stir, then cover the dish and cook on full power for 10 minutes.

Add seasoning to taste, the prawns, mussels and peas to the paella. Stir lightly, re-cover and continue to cook on high for a further 10 minutes. Add the tomatoes to the paella just before serving.

VARIATIONS

Paella is a dish that should contain a variety of seafood as well as chicken, a plentiful portion of vegetables and the essential saffron. Cook some fresh mussels (see page 110) in the microwave and add them to the paella instead of the frozen ones. Reserve a few in shells to add as a garnish. The vegetables used can include French beans, carrots and sliced celery. For additional colour add a few whole cooked prawns and some wedges of lemon as a garnish.

RISOTTO

SERVES 4

You can add all sorts of ingredients to this dish as shown below. Try a variety of vegetables, sliced continental sausages, diced cooked chicken or ham, or grated cheese.

1 large onion, chopped
1 green pepper, deseeded and
   chopped
1 head fennel, trimmed and
   chopped
3 tablespoons olive oil
2 cloves garlic, crushed

600 ml/1 pint chicken stock
   (page 108)
salt and freshly ground black
   pepper
225 g/8 oz long-grain rice
plenty of grated Parmesan
   cheese to serve

Place the vegetables in a large casserole dish with the oil and garlic. Cover and cook on high for 5 minutes. Stir in the stock and a little seasoning. Add the rice.

   Cover and cook on high for 20 minutes, or until the liquid has been absorbed. Fluff up the grains and serve with plenty of Parmesan cheese.

Risotto

Kedgeree

KEDGEREE

SERVES 4

1 large onion, chopped
50 g/2 oz butter
grated rind of 1 lemon
$\frac{1}{2}$ teaspoon turmeric
pinch of curry powder
225 g/8 oz long-grain rice
600 ml/1 pint boiling water

salt and freshly ground black
   pepper
450 g/1 lb smoked haddock,
   skinned and cut into chunks
2 tablespoons chopped parsley
4 hard-boiled eggs, roughly
   chopped

Put the onion and butter in a casserole dish and cook on full power for 3 minutes. Stir in the lemon rind, spices and rice. Pour in the water and add seasoning. Cover and cook on full power for 10 minutes. Stir lightly, then add the fish, without stirring it in, and re-cover the dish. Cook on high for a further 5–10 minutes, or until the fish is cooked and the majority of the water absorbed. Stir in the parsley and eggs and serve.

ADDITIONAL INGREDIENTS
You may like to try using the following ingredients, some to replace certain items, others to add to the dish.
Use smoked mackerel instead of smoked haddock, adding it 5 minutes before the end of the cooking time.
Add 50 g/2 oz roughly chopped salted peanuts.
Add 50 g/2 oz sultanas, raisins or currants.
Omit the spices and cook with a bay leaf; remove the bay leaf before serving.
Add 100 g/4 oz sliced mushrooms.

◆ SAUCES

GRAVY OR WINE SAUCE

SERVES 4–6

meat or poultry cooking juices
3–4 tablespoons plain flour
600 ml/1 pint boiling stock,
    water or wine

salt and freshly ground black
    pepper

Drain excess fat from the meat juices, then stir in the flour and whisk in the stock, water, red or white wine. If you are using water or wine you may like to add a stock cube or a little tomato or vegetable purée. Season to taste and cook on high for 10 minutes. Whisk well, then serve.

BOLOGNAISE SAUCE

SERVES 4

Serve this meat sauce with pasta – spaghetti, lasagne or other shapes – or use it in cottage pie or to fill plain pancakes.

1 large onion, chopped
225 g/8 oz carrots, diced
1 green pepper, deseeded and
    chopped
2 cloves garlic, crushed
2 tablespoons oil
2 tablespoons plain flour
450 g/1 lb minced beef

bay leaf
1 (425-g/15-oz) can tomatoes
2 tablespoons tomato purée
300 ml/½ pint beef stock or red
    wine
salt and freshly ground black
    pepper
2 tablespoons chopped parsley

Put the onion, carrot, pepper and garlic in a casserole dish with the oil. Cover and cook on high for 5 minutes. Stir in all the remaining ingredients except the parsley and cover the dish.

    Cook on high for 10 minutes, stir well, then cook for a further 10–15 minutes. Leave to stand for 2 minutes. Add the parsley and serve.

BREAD SAUCE

SERVES 4

Serve this sauce with roast poultry or boiled or baked ham.

1 large onion
6 cloves
bay leaf
600 ml/1 pint milk

100 g/4 oz fresh breadcrumbs
salt and freshly ground black
    pepper
a little grated nutmeg

Stud the onion with the cloves and place it in a large basin. Cover and cook on high for 2 minutes. Add the bay leaf and milk, re-cover and continue to cook on high for 6–6½ minutes.

    Stir in the remaining ingredients and cook on high for 2 minutes. Scoop the onion and bay leaf out of the sauce. Whisk well and serve.

BÉCHAMEL SAUCE

MAKES 600 ml/1 PINT

40 g/1½ oz plain flour
600 ml/1 pint milk
bay leaf

blade of mace
salt and pepper
knob of butter

Put the flour in a basin large enough to allow room for the sauce to boil up as it cooks. Gradually whisk in the milk, making sure that the mixture is smooth. Add the bay leaf and mace, seasoning and butter. Cook using microwaves only on high for 3 minutes. Whisk thoroughly, then cook for a further 5 minutes and whisk again. Cook on high for a further 1–3 minutes, until the sauce has boiled and thickened. Whisk well to remove any lumps, then taste and adjust the seasoning before serving.

VARIATIONS

Omit the bay leaf and mace from the above recipe and add the following ingredients:

Parsley Sauce Add 4–6 tablespoons chopped parsley to the sauce just before serving. Serve with fish or boiled ham.
Cheese Sauce Add 100 g/4 oz grated matured Cheddar cheese and 2 teaspoons prepared mustard to the sauce about 3 minutes before the end of the cooking time. Whisk well, then finish cooking as above. Serve with fish, vegetables, eggs or pasta.
Egg Sauce Add 4 chopped hard-boiled eggs to the sauce at the end of the cooking time. Serve with fish, pasta or vegetables.

ONION SAUCE

MAKES 600 ml/1 PINT

1 large (Spanish) onion or 2
    medium onions, finely
    chopped
25 g/1 oz butter

40 g/1½ oz plain flour
600 ml/1 pint milk
salt and pepper
bay leaf

Put the onion and butter in a large basin allowing room for the sauce to boil up as it cooks. Cook using microwaves only on high for 4 minutes. Stir in the flour, then gradually whisk in the milk, making sure that there are no lumps of flour left in the sauce. Add a little seasoning and the bay leaf.

    Continue to cook on high for 3 minutes, then whisk thoroughly and cook for a further 5 minutes. Whisk again and cook for 1–2 minutes or until the sauce boils and thickens. Taste and adjust the seasoning before serving with ham, grilled meats and sausages, vegetables or pasta.

VARIATION

Mushroom Sauce Use 175 g/6 oz sliced button mushrooms instead of the onion. Cook as above. Serve with grilled meats, grilled fish or pasta. This sauce can be enriched by substituting 2–4 tablespoons dry sherry or cream for an equal quantity of the milk.

TOMATO SAUCE

MAKES 600 ml / 1 PINT

1 onion, chopped
1 small carrot, chopped
1 stick celery, chopped
2 cloves garlic, crushed
25 g/1 oz butter or 2
    tablespoons oil
bay leaf

salt and freshly ground black
    pepper
$\frac{1}{2}$ teaspoon dried thyme
2 (397-g/14-oz) cans chopped
    tomatoes
150 ml/$\frac{1}{4}$ pint red wine

Put the onion, carrot and celery in a large basin with the garlic and butter or oil. Mix well, cover and cook using microwaves only on high for 5 minutes. Add the bay leaf and seasoning. Stir in the thyme and tomatoes, then pour in the red wine. Re-cover and cook on high for a further 8 minutes.

Blend the sauce in a liquidiser or press it through a fine sieve. Reheat on high for 2 minutes before serving.

Serve with fish, meat, vegetables, rice or pasta.

HOLLANDAISE SAUCE

SERVES 4

This is a rich sauce using plenty of butter and eggs. Serve it with fish or vegetables.

2 tablespoons lemon juice
1 tablespoon water
2 large egg yolks

salt and freshly ground black
    pepper
100 g/4 oz butter

Place the lemon juice and water in a basin. Cook on high for about 3–5 minutes. At the end of the cooking time the liquid should be reduced to about 1 tablespoon. The time will vary with the individual oven. Whisk in the egg yolks immediately the liquid is removed from the oven. Add a little seasoning and set aside.

Put the butter in a basin and heat on high for 2–2$\frac{1}{2}$ minutes, until melted and quite hot. Whisking all the time, add the butter in a slow trickle to the eggs.

Cook on high for a further 30–60 seconds, stir well and serve at once.

CRANBERRY SAUCE

SERVES 4–6

Serve with turkey.

100 g/4 oz cranberries
75 g/3 oz sugar
2 tablespoons port

Put the cranberries and sugar in a basin, cover and cook on high for 3 minutes. Stir in the port and leave to cool.

APPLE SAUCE

SERVES 4–6

Serve with roast pork, baked or boiled ham, or roast goose.

450 g/1 lb cooking apples,
    peeled, cored and sliced

75 g/3 oz sugar
25 g/1 oz butter

Put the apples and sugar in a casserole dish or basin and cover. Cook on high for 5–7 minutes. Beat well, adding the butter. Serve cold.

CUSTARD SAUCE

MAKES 600 ml / 1 PINT

This is a compromise between a traditional egg custard and custard made using just custard powder.

2 tablespoons custard powder
2 egg yolks

2 tablespoons sugar
600 ml/1 pint milk

Mix the custard powder with the egg yolks and sugar, adding just enough of the milk to make a smooth, thick cream. Heat the rest of the milk in a large basin on high for 4 minutes.

Whisking all the time, gradually pour the milk on to the custard powder mixture. Pour the custard back into the basin and cook on high for 2–4 minutes, whisking once during cooking. The custard should be slightly thickened and smooth. Serve hot with fruit pies and other puddings.

BRANDY SAUCE

MAKES 600 ml / 1 PINT

Serve with Christmas pudding, pies, steamed puddings or baked puddings.

3 tablespoons cornflour
3 tablespoons sugar

450 ml/$\frac{3}{4}$ pint milk
150 ml/$\frac{1}{4}$ pint brandy

In a basin mix the cornflour with the sugar and a little of the milk until smooth. Gradually whisk in the remaining milk and cook on high for 5 minutes.

Whisk thoroughly, then cook for a further 4 minutes, or until the sauce boils and thickens. Whisk thoroughly, then whisk in the brandy and heat for 1 minute. Serve hot.

◆ DESSERTS

STEAMED SPONGE PUDDING

SERVES 4

50 g/2 oz soft margarine | 50 g/2 oz self-raising flour
50 g/2 oz sugar | 2 tablespoons milk
1 egg | 4 tablespoons jam

Put all the ingredients apart from the jam in a basin and beat thoroughly until well combined, creamy and pale. Use an electric mixer if possible.

Put the jam in the bottom of a greased 1.15-litre/2-pint basin. Spoon the sponge mixture on top and spread it out evenly. Cook on high for 4–5 minutes. Leave to stand for 5 minutes before turning out. Serve hot.

CARAMELISED ORANGES

SERVES 4

175 g/6 oz sugar
6 tablespoons water
4 large oranges

Put the sugar and water in a large basin or casserole dish. Cook on high for 2 minutes. Stir well, then continue to cook for a further 8–10 minutes. Keep a close eye on the caramel to prevent it from overcooking. Remove the dish from the oven when the caramel is a pale golden colour.

Meanwhile, cut all the peel and pith off the oranges. Slice the fruit and remove the pips. Overlap the orange slices in a heatproof serving dish and pour the cooked caramel over. Leave until cool, then chill thoroughly.

◆ If you like, pare thin strips of orange rind from the whole oranges first. Cut into fine shreds and put in a basin with hot water. Cook on high for 3–5 minutes, then drain and sprinkle over the prepared fruit before adding the caramel.

Crème Caramel

CRÈME CARAMEL

SERVES 4

Caramel | 5 teaspoons sugar
100 g/4 oz sugar | 350 ml/12 fl oz milk
4 tablespoons water | a few drops of vanilla essence
Custard
2 small eggs

Put the sugar and water in a basin and cook on high for 2 minutes. Stir well, then continue to cook on high for a further 9–11 minutes, or until the caramel is a pale golden colour. Take care that the caramel does not overcook and watch it closely towards the end of the time.

Divide the caramel between four ramekins. Hold them with an oven glove or tea-towel and swirl the caramel round the sides. Set aside.

Beat the eggs with the sugar, then add the milk and vanilla essence. Strain into the dishes. Stand the ramekins in a flan dish, then put it in the microwave and pour in boiling water to come halfway up the flan dish. Cook on high for 3–3½ minutes. The custard should be very lightly set. Turn the dishes once during cooking. Cool, then chill overnight. Turn out on to individual plates and serve.

LEMON FLUFF

SERVES 4

You can decorate this dessert with coarsely grated citrus rind.

grated rind and juice of 3 lemons	cold water
50 g/2 oz sugar	150 ml/¼ pint single cream
25 g/1 oz cornflour	2 egg whites

Mix the lemon rind and juice in a large measuring jug with the sugar and cornflour until smooth and creamy. Make up to 300 ml/½ pint with water. Cook on high for 3 minutes, then whisk well and cook for a further 3 minutes, or until the sauce boils and becomes very thick. Beat thoroughly, then gradually beat in the cream and set aside for a few minutes until cooled to warm.

 Whisk the egg whites until they stand in stiff peaks. Stir a spoonful of egg white into the lemon mixture, then carefully fold in the rest. Divide between four individual dishes and chill for about 1 hour. Serve with crisp sweet biscuits.

Lemon Fluff

GOOSEBERRY FOOL

SERVES 6

The microwave is great for cooking fruit which is to be puréed for use in a fool. Try cooking blackcurrants, blackberries, cherries, plums and apricots.

675 g/1½ lb gooseberries, topped and tailed	450 ml/¾ pint double cream or whipping cream
225 g/8 oz sugar	

Put the gooseberries in a casserole dish or bowl with the sugar. Cover and cook on high for 5 minutes. Stir well then cook for a further 5 minutes. Leave to cool slightly before blending in a liquidiser until smooth. Press through a sieve to remove the seeds.

 Whip the cream until thick, then fold it into the fruit purée. Spoon into six glass dishes and chill well before serving.

PEARS IN RED WINE

SERVES 4

This is a very basic dessert recipe – you can vary it by using cider instead of wine, by adding grated orange rind for additional flavour or by adding a few raisins, chopped dried apricots or dates. Serve hot or chilled with cream.

4 large, firm pears, peeled and cored	150 ml/¼ pint red wine
a little lemon juice	1 cinnamon stick
75 g/3 oz sugar	4 cloves

Put the pears in a casserole dish and sprinkle with lemon juice to prevent them from discolouring. Add the sugar and pour in the wine. Stir well, adding the cinnamon stick and cloves.

 Cover the dish and cook on high for 5 minutes. Stir, rearrange the pears and cook for a further 5 minutes. Baste the pears once or twice during cooking. Serve hot, removing the cinnamon stick and cloves, or cool and chill.

◆ DEFROSTING AND REHEATING

The magic of microwaves is captured in the processes of defrosting and reheating foods. Never before has there been an appliance that enables you to take food from the freezer and turn it into a piping hot meal in minutes rather than hours. It really is amazing, when you first use a microwave oven, to watch a plate of food heat quickly, without ruining the flavour and texture and without the plate becoming baking hot.

The timings given here are intended as a guide – use your judgement in deciding when food needs turning over or rearranging, or just when it has defrosted sufficiently for cooking. At first you will have to pay careful attention to the food as it defrosts but as you become familiar with your own oven, then you will be a better judge of the timings and will find it unnecessary to calculate defrosting times in the greatest detail.

Aim to microwave the food until it is still slightly icy, then allow it to stand for a while until it has defrosted completely. If you are defrosting large pieces of dense food (for example a large joint of meat), then it is a good idea to leave them to stand for 5–10 minutes in the middle of the defrosting time.

Defrosting Cooked Soups, Casseroles and Sauces

First put the container in the microwave (remove food from metal containers or remove any metal lids) and cook on defrost for 3–5 minutes, or until the contents can be released into a suitable dish or bowl. Then give the food a brief burst on high microwave setting – the time will depend on the quantity of food, but about 3–5 minutes is a guide. Gently break up the food as far as possible, then continue defrosting on defrost setting, in spurts of about 5–7 minutes, depending on quantity. Break up and rearrange the block of food as it defrosts. Once the food has virtually defrosted it can be reheated on a medium or high microwave setting.

Reheating Plated Meals

The arrangement of the food on the plate can be important in determining the success of this method. Put dense foods that take a lot of reheating towards the outside of the plate. Put light ingredients – slices of meat, for example – towards the middle of the plate. Coat carved meat in gravy or sauce to prevent drying out. Use a special microwave plate-stacker to reheat two or more plated meals. The following times are a guide to reheating on **high**:

1 plated meal _____ 3–5 minutes
(*meat and two vegetables with gravy or sauce*)
Steak and kidney pie _____ 1½–2 minutes
(*Individual size*)
1 slice of quiche _____ 45–60 seconds
Individual cottage pie _____ 5–8 minutes
(*depending on size*)
Bolognese sauce on pasta _____ 4–5 minutes

USEFUL TIPS

● *Defrosting or softening butter that has been in the refrigerator* Unwrap and put in suitable dish or plate. Microwave on high for a few seconds, a little longer if frozen.

● *Warming chilled cheese* To bring refrigerated cheese to room temperature for serving, put on plate and microwave on high for a few seconds.

● *Melting chocolate* Break into pieces and place in basin. Melt on high for 1–2 minutes, then stir well. If melting large quantities use a medium setting to avoid overheating any areas of the chocolate before other pieces have melted.

● *Heating small portions of food for baby or toddler* Put straight in suitable dish and heat for a minute, then stir well and test to see if further heating is required. Take care to stir well to eliminate any hot spots and do not overheat.

● *Blanching vegetables before freezing* Place vegetables in roasting bag with a little water. Cook briefly, then plunge them into iced water and drain immediately. Pack, label and freeze.

● *Heating individual cups of coffee or milky drinks* Put in microwave and heat on high for 1–2 minutes, or a little longer depending on size of cup. Stir well.

● *Softening butter or margarine for creaming* A few seconds on high is long enough.

● *Warming bread or rolls* Place straight in a napkin-lined basket and heat on high for a few minutes.

DEFROSTING FISH AND SEAFOOD

	DEFROSTING TIME PER 450 g/1 lb IN MINUTES ON DEFROST SETTING	DEFROSTING INSTRUCTIONS
Fish Fillets	5–6	Separate the fillets as soon as they are sufficiently defrosted. Turn over and rearrange if necessary halfway through.
Fish Steaks	6–7	Turn halfway through. The steaks should be arranged with the thicker part towards the outside of the dish.
Whole fish	6–7	Turn halfway through defrosting. Rinse and dry the body cavity before cooking.
Prawns (peeled, cooked)	4–5	Place in a basin. Stir halfway through defrosting. Drain and turn on to absorbent kitchen paper. Rub off any remaining ice gently to leave slightly icy prawns.

DEFROSTING POULTRY

Whole chicken or duck	5–6	Remove outer wrapping and place on flan dish. Turn twice during defrosting. If joint tips begin to cook, cover with small pieces of cooking foil. Remove giblets and rinse body cavity to remove any traces of ice. Leave to stand 10 minutes before cooking.
Whole turkey	5–7	Remove wrapping and put in flan dish as above. Turn several times during defrosting. Shield protruding bones with cooking foil to prevent cooking. Halfway through defrosting leave to stand for 10 minutes. Allow to stand for a further 15 minutes before cooking. Remove giblets and rinse body cavity.
Chicken pieces (or other poultry joints and portions)	5–7	Arrange pieces in dish with any thick parts towards the outside. Turn and rearrange halfway through defrosting, then leave to stand 5–10 minutes before cooking.

DEFROSTING MEAT

Joints, on the bone (for example, leg or shoulder of lamb, rib of beef, leg of pork)	4–5	Unwrap the meat and place on a flan dish. Turn several times during defrosting and shield any areas that are likely to overcook with small pieces of cooking foil. The bone conducts heat to the meat. Leave very large joints to stand for 10 minutes halfway through. Stand all joints 15–20 minutes at end of defrosting time.
Joints, off the bone (for example, rolled rib, topside or brisket, rolled breast of lamb, loin of pork or leg of pork)	5–7	As above.
Minced meat	6–8	Unwrap and place in dish. Break up and turn as the meat begins to defrost. When still icy leave 10 minutes before use.
Chops	5–7	Defrosting time depends on thickness. Separate, if necessary, during defrosting. Turn over once or twice. Stand 10–15 minutes.
Sausages	5–7	Unwrap and put on plate. Separate as soon as possible and arrange as far apart as possible. Stand 5 minutes.

DEFROSTING BREAD

Small loaf (unsliced)	3–5	Unwrap bread if necessary. Place on absorbent kitchen paper on a plate or put straight into oven. Turn over halfway through, then stand 10–15 minutes.
Large loaf (unsliced)	7–9	As above.
Bread rolls		Place on absorbent kitchen paper as far apart as possible in the oven. Leave to stand for 2–3 minutes.
–1	30 seconds	
–2	45–60 seconds	
–3	$1\frac{1}{2}$	
–4	$2–2\frac{1}{2}$	
Sliced bread		Separate slices as soon as possible and arrange on absorbent kitchen paper straight in oven. Rearrange as necessary halfway through.
–1	30 seconds	
–2	1	
–3	$1\frac{1}{2}–2$	
–4	$2\frac{1}{2}–3$	

◆ INDEX ◆

◆ INDEX